Raised to Serve, Selected to Lead

Raised to Serve, Selected to Lead
Lessons for New Military and Civilian Leaders

Robert F. Griffin, MD

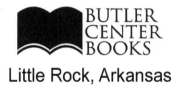

BUTLER
CENTER
BOOKS

Little Rock, Arkansas

The Butler Center for Arkansas Studies

BUTLER
CENTER
BOOKS

Central Arkansas Library System
100 Rock Street
Little Rock, Arkansas 72201
www.butlercenter.org

March 2019
ISBN 978-1-945624-23-0

Book and cover design: Mike Keckhaver
Copyeditor: Ali Welky

Cataloging-in-Publication data is on file at the Library of Congress
Names: Griffin, Robert F., author.
Title: Raised to serve, selected to lead:
lessons for new military and civilian leaders/Robert F. Griffin, MD.
Description: Little Rock, Arkansas : Butler Center Books, 2019.
Identifiers: LCCN 2018055837 | ISBN 9781945624230 (hardcover : alk. paper)
Subjects: LCSH: Griffin, Robert F. | Leadership. | Leadership--Study and
teaching--United States. | Arkansas Blue Cross and Blue
Shield--Employees--Biography. | Generals--United States--Biography. |
United States. Army--Surgeons--Biography. | United States. Army. Medical
Brigade, 332nd--Biography. | Families of military personnel--United
States--Biography.
Classification: LCC HD57.7 .G753 2019 | DDC 355.0092 [B] --dc23
LC record available at https://lccn.loc.gov/2018055837

Butler Center Books, the publishing division of the
Butler Center for Arkansas Studies,
was made possible by the generosity of
Dora Johnson Ragsdale and John G. Ragsdale Jr.

Special thanks to Arkansas Blue Cross and Blue Shield for underwriting
the publication of this book, in honor of Dr. Robert F. Griffin.

Printed in the United States of America

Cover photos courtesy of the author

Dedications

To my parents Colonel Linwood Griffin Jr. and Zelda Crocker Griffin, now deceased, for their sacrifices in raising me and my siblings with a burning desire to be of service to our country.

To Captain David O. Treadwell for his leadership of B Company, 4th Battalion, 21st Infantry preparing us for combat in the jungles of Hawaii; First Lieutenant José (Joe) Pena, my West Point classmate who was killed covering my right flank in close combat near Tam Ky, Vietnam; Platoon Sergeant Morales Torres for his sage advice and support during months of combat operations in Vietnam, culminating with my final battle near Tam Ky; and particularly Staff Sergeant Nicky D. Bacon, who was awarded the Medal of Honor for his actions in saving my life and the lives of other members of my platoon who were wounded and trapped forward of the enemy bunker line, and for rallying the remainder of my platoon and Joe's platoon; and also to the medical soldiers who cared for me through my recovery and encouraged me to attend medical school, join the Army Medical Department, and care for soldiers for the remainder of my career. To the radio-telephone operators (RTOs) of the Light Infantry, particularly Dale Walls (mine), Ed Gross (Captain Treadwell's), and Kirby Demumbreum (Joe's). These brave soldiers were always within about eight feet of each of us and shared every risk without expecting credit for doing so. The Viet Cong were known to identify RTOs by their antennas and shoot the person closest to them first (most likely an officer or senior NCO) and then shoot the RTO. In addition, it was not uncommon for the Viet Cong to put a trip wire high so it would be caught by an RTO's antenna and trigger an improvised explosive device to kill the RTO and all in proximity of him.

To Major General Paul J. Vanderploog, whose guidance, philosophy of leadership, and mentoring were critical to my success (I quote him frequently in this book). When I took command of the Third Medical Battalion (3d MED BN) in 1984, I had not commanded any unit since I turned over command of an infantry training company in 1970, fourteen years before, with an entirely different structure, minimal equipment, and a narrow mission. Meanwhile, the Army had changed considerably and was far more complex. Further, I had no experience with the logistical and maintenance requirements of a medical battalion with multiple trucks, generators, and items of equipment, a deficit which was compounded when we acquired fifteen armored, tracked ambulances. Fortunately, I had a great staff under Major Gary Kindred's leadership, and (then) Colonel Vanderploog was an incredible teacher. The lessons that I learned from him have served me well and are a major component of this book.

To Major General Mike Strong and the 332 Medical Brigade staff and units that were deployed to a combat zone for a mission for which they were not designed, staffed, or previously equipped to accomplish, yet did so with distinction. The brigade was composed of U.S. Army Reserve, Army National Guard, and Regular Army units from Europe and multiple states, with variable training and readiness levels, with attached units with little or no collective training with each other, and with limited or no experience with the new hospital system they were to employ for the first time in a combat environment. Nevertheless, by the onset of the ground war in Iraq and Kuwait, medical units had overcome these obstacles and were staffed and ready.

To all of the men and women of our uniformed services who stand ready every day around the world to make sure that wars are either deterred or fought in other lands and not in the United States and Canada.

To my wife, Ann, for her previous service as an Army nurse and her encouragement and support as we moved twelve times on active duty and twice in retirement. She made everywhere we lived better through her innumerable contributions to the community with participation and leadership in volunteer activities wherever life took us, and for raising and endowing our children with a commitment for service to others and to our country.

To the next generation of our family: Daniel and Darlene with Olivia, Alexia, and Hunter in Florida; Major (USAF) Carolyn and Michael Carmody with Cecilia, James, Felicity, and Mackenzie currently stationed at Joint Base San Antonio-Fort Sam Houston, Texas; Dr. Laura and Major (USAF) Marion Carter currently stationed in Virginia with Damien; and Captains (USAR) Tom and Sarah Griffin currently at the University of Vermont—and any more grandchildren that may arrive. Through them, a family legacy of leadership and service to community and country will endure well into the future.

Table of Contents

Abbreviations and Vocabulary

AN .... Army Nurse Corps

ARNG .... Army National Guard

BDE .... Brigade (three or more battalion-sized units commanded by a COL or BG)

BG .... Brigadier General

BN .... Battalion (500–700 soldiers commanded by an LTC)

C&GSC .... Command and General Staff College (one-year course to prepare for LTC positions)

CG .... Commanding General

CN .... Chief Nurse

COL .... Colonel

Corps .... Combination of two or more divisions with the associated support structure commanded by an LTG identified by Roman numeral (as in VII Corps)

CPT .... Captain

CSM .... Command Sergeant Major

DCA .... Deputy Commander for Administration

DCCS .... Deputy Commander for Clinical Services

DCN .... Deputy Commander for Nursing

GEN .... General

ID .... Infantry Division (15,000 to 20,000 soldiers commanded by an MG)

IOBC .... Officers Basic Course (OBC) is an initial branch-specific course to make sure all new officers have the basic foundation of a specific branch. (The letter I refers to Infantry.)

Kaserne .... German for "barracks"

LIB .... Light Infantry Brigade

LT .... Lieutenant, 1LT and 2LT

LTC .... Lieutenant Colonel

LTG .... Lieutenant General

MAJ .... Major

MC .... Medical Corps

MEDCOM .... Medical Command

MG .... Major General

MS .... Medical Service Corps

PCS .... Permanent Change of Station

POV .... Privately owned vehicle

PX or BX .... Post (Army) or Base (Air Force) Exchange (department store)

Quarters .... Military family housing

RGT .... Regiment (historical designation for certain combat arms units)

RTO .... Radio-telephone operator

SSC .... Senior Service College such as Army War College (one-year course to prepare officers for COL and higher assignments)

USAF .... U.S. Air Force

USAR .... U.S. Army Reserve

USMA .... U.S. Military Academy or West Point

Foreword

As time goes by, the memories we make distill themselves into a handful of recollections, the events by which we define who we were at various points in our past. Bob Griffin's stories are more dramatic than most: a childhood spent in a military family traveling the world; the rigors of West Point; a nearly fatal war wound, although "nearly fatal" may be too tame to describe the realization of having been placed with the dead who a short time before had been his comrades; months of convalescence; medical school and a general surgery residency; ascending through the Army ranks to become a General Officer; organizing the medical preparation for another war; and a return to the very complicated world of civilian medicine in America. But for Bob, these events were not moments to remember; they were events preparing him for leadership. When I first met Bob, we quickly found a bond as two old veterans of a long-ago war. But I soon realized that he views past experience differently than most of us. More than anyone I have ever known, he has motivated himself throughout his life even in times of great personal hardship to learn from his own leadership successes and failures and those of the people around him. Fortunately, this wisdom and the stories from which it came are now shared in this book.

—Vic Snyder, 2018

Vic Snyder is a U.S. Marine Corps veteran, family physician, and lawyer who served seven terms in the U.S. Congress representing Arkansas's Second Congressional District. Snyder currently serves as corporate medical director for external affairs with Arkansas Blue Cross and Blue Shield.

Acknowledgments

The idea to write this book was not my own. Rather, after lectures on leadership that I had given to emerging leaders at Arkansas Blue Cross and Blue Shield (ABCBS), I was approached by Dr. Victor Snyder, a former U.S. congressman who was serving as corporate medical director for external affairs at Arkansas Blue and Cross Blue Shield, with the suggestion that I share my story, combining my personal history with the leadership lessons I had learned over the years. I thanked him for his kind comments regarding my talks and went on about my business without giving it much thought. However, Vic soon invited me to visit the Butler Center for Arkansas Studies and to meet with David Stricklin, the director. Together, they convinced me that I should give this serious consideration and conducted oral history interviews to assist me with my thoughts. This book is the direct result of their constant encouragement, and I am grateful to them and the staff at the Butler Center, including Rod Lorenzen, Ali Welky, and Michael Keckhaver, for making this a reality.

The mission of the United States Army in simple terms is to deter war, but if need be, to fight and win. Since the expense of maintaining a standing Army of a size and strength for a major conflict of substantial duration is greater than our political process would be expected to permit, implicit in this mission is the potential requirement for rapid expansion. Identification of leadership potential and leader development are mission-essential tasks, not just for current operations, but for future potential threats. I was first identified as having potential worth developing by Captain David Treadwell, my company commander in Hawaii and Vietnam, with the concurrence of then Lieutenant Colonel James Armstrong, my battalion commander. Later, this was reinforced by then Major General William R. Richardson, and this led to my early selection for Command and General Staff College and brought me to the attention of Lieutenant General Bernard Mittemeyer, the Army Surgeon General, who charted my path from there.

My success as a leader was not purely based upon my efforts, but rather, it must be attributed to the actions of those whom I led and the performance of those they led. Consequently, in writing this, I have attributed the lessons to the leaders from whom I have learned the more crucial lessons, but I have fallen short in identifying many of those who actually demonstrated their value through their actions and leadership in the brilliant execution of my requests. I have relied on the efforts of so many leaders below me in the chain of command or organizational structure that I cannot possibly list them all, but with apologies to those I may have failed to mention, I would like to specifically mention those who have been absolutely critical to my success.

- Bob Davie, Dean Kunihiro, and Tom Condon, who were my roommates at West Point, for always shining a bright light on a dark day
- The late LTC (Retired) Richard Helmbold, MS, for being my best supporter and trusted guide as I transitioned from Infantry Officer to Medical Corps leader
- Captain John Singler (Canal Zone) and Lieutenant Jim Ross (Canal Zone and Saudi Arabia) for excellence in field medical training, operations, and logistics
- Command Sergeant Majors Richard Sirois (3d MED BN), Lawrence Williams (98th GEN HOSP), Gary Terry (West Point) and Chin Wang (Dwight David Eisenhower Army Medical Center or DDEAMC) for maintaining the highest standards for soldier appearance, training, and discipline through personal example and counseling, and for their timely and sound advice regarding soldier requirements
- Colonels Johnny and Jo Rusin for advising and assisting me in my roles as VII Corps and FORSCOM Command Surgeon
- Colonel Charles H. Champion, Deputy Army Forces Command (FORSCOM) Surgeon, for sage advice and professional staff support
- Colonels Bill Bester and Lester Martinez for outstanding leadership and execution of my guidance while commanding the Army Community Hospitals at Fort Jackson and Fort Campbell
- Colonels Paul Brooke and Jim Eason (98th GEN HOSP), Paul Holland (332 MED BDE), Lynn Wal-

ton (West Point), David Rubenstein (DDEAMC), and George Masi (SERMC) for being outstanding MS leaders who provided strong administrative and logistical oversight to these complex organizations

- Colonels Ernest Sutton (98th GEN HOSP) and Walter Moore (DDEAMC) for their oversight of the professional staff at these organizations to ensure the highest level of responsiveness and quality of healthcare services, actually drawing patients from other military health services areas
- Colonels Patricia Wise and Maryann Steinmetz (DDE-AMC) for outstanding nursing leadership creating and sustaining an environment of the highest quality of nursing service with a strong commitment to serving patients' needs above all others. Both were outstanding professionals and a credit to their profession.
- Dr. Steve Perkins recruited me to BCBSVT and taught me the fundamentals of insurance-based medical management, while RNs Mary Ann Purnell and Linda Lou showed me how health-plan-based case management nurses can reach out to covered individuals, assess their knowledge and behavior, and leverage these to support and encourage them as they strive to improve their health status and decrease their health costs.

Preface

In construction engineering, one quickly learns that it is essential to build a solid foundation before proceeding to the upper levels. There are multiple methods for the design and construction of a foundation that will meet the requirements of the final product, but the foundation must suit the purpose and be solidly built. A solid foundation does not guarantee against eventual structural failure, however, particularly if the components may degrade over time, a defective foundation inevitably leads to early failure. The requirement for a solid foundation applies to human endeavors as well, and it especially applies to leaders. This is particularly true in circumstances that require the demonstration of a moral authority to lead if others are to follow.

As in engineering, there are many ways to build a person's foundation, and each foundation is unique to an individual. As with structures, weaknesses are not always readily apparent. A superficial inspection will not tell if the concrete was mixed properly with the correct components, nor whether it is appropriately reinforced with properly hardened steel. Similarly, values encompassing morality, ethics, religious foundation and tolerance of others, integrity, interpersonal relationships, and societal expectations can be masked. Only time will tell, though circumstances will eventually reveal those with a solid foundation and those who succumb to weaknesses. Some deficits can be repaired, but this is no easy task. It takes a substantial and conscientious personal effort combined with a willingness to recognize, accept, confront, and reflect upon one's own shortfalls, as well as a high degree of self-discipline, to repair and strengthen one's own foundation beyond adolescence. This must be a continuous, lifetime effort. It can be done, and it is never too late to start. This is particularly true in military service.

This book is in three sections. The first describes the development of my particular foundation, but this is fundamentally a tribute to the men, women, and families of the U.S. Armed Forces in the late 1940s through the mid-1960s. The characters and behaviors of these people helped me develop a solid foundation, and I give insights into their lives and those of us who grew up in their shadow. It is the story of my parents in the service of our country, and my siblings and me as we accompanied them on my father's many assignments around the globe. It tells what my parents, and their colleagues and families, endured in the service of our nation. Since this is the foundation upon which I built my careers and which influenced my early decision making, it seems appropriate to relate how I entered the path to become a leader in both the military and corporate America.

The second section begins as I enter the U.S. Military Academy (USMA) and describes what I learned as I progressed in my subsequent careers. It is a tribute to my family and the truly great leaders with whom I had the privilege to serve and who mentored me from their experiences along the way, many of which are similar to my own, as I was raised in an Army family. Of necessity, this will include explanations of the structure of the U.S. Army and civilian organizations, and will provide introductions of the leaders who I have attempted to emulate.

The third section consists of associated leadership lessons that primarily reflect my own observations and thoughts. In it I present my recommendations for consideration by anyone choosing the path to become a leader.

I believe that there are five fundamental elements of learning: reading, listening, observing, practicing, and reflecting. While many, particularly academicians, learn best from reading or from lectures, I have found that I learn best through observation. While I have benefited from study, lectures, training sessions, and seminars pertaining to leadership, the style which I developed is primarily attributable to the observation of great leaders in action—but also upon my observation and analysis of the few truly abysmal leaders I have encountered. Observing how not to lead can almost be as powerful as observing successful leaders.

The characteristics that I promote here are those which I adopted from observing the leadership techniques or styles of the admirable leaders I have observed. My personal success and contributions as a leader are directly attributable to my willingness to adopt the leadership elements which I selected from those who served above me, with me, or below me in different environments and organizations. I certainly did not start my career as an accomplished leader. In fact, I think that I had the dedication and determination, but my skills were moderate at best. However, throughout my careers, I drew upon the strengths of others in order to recognize my shortcomings and evolve, and I was successful through a constant effort to refine and improve my leadership philosophy, principles, and style.

Because what I accomplished and will relate is not a story of some intrinsic talent, but rather a highlighting of what I observed and adopted from these great leaders in action, it is important that I credit them for my successes. Where I can attribute a specific positive characteristic to an identifiable source, I will acknowledge and give credit to that individual.

Along the way, my service also provided me with the far more painful opportunity to observe a fair number of mediocre and poor leaders and to witness, struggle with, and attempt to attenuate the impact upon morale and productivity that they generated. I have reflected as much upon behavior demonstrated by them and the mediocrity, discord, and discontent sown by the weaker leaders as I have upon the great ones. However, when I share the negative lessons one should be aware of, I will endeavor to mask these individuals' identity.

Also, since much of my biography is a matter of public record, and I have been fortunate to have served with far more great leaders than poor ones, I want to make it clear that not specifically mentioning one of my former leaders, peers, or followers by name does not mean someone was a poor leader. Rather, so many of these impressive leaders exhibited the same or similar positive traits that they reinforced and strengthened what I had already observed. Since I cannot possibly recognize them all, I have identified either the ones who made the earliest impression or had the greatest impact in developing me as a leader.

I found it useful to take note of each of the lessons and to apply the ones that I could incorporate into my personal leadership style as it developed and evolved over time. I particularly made note of those which could be reduced to "sound bites" I could use both to remind myself as to what I wanted to accomplish and to share with others. I reviewed the lessons frequently, added to them as the opportunities were presented, and evaluated myself on the degree to which I consistently applied the lessons that I learned.

Whenever I felt that I had dealt with a situation or person in a manner not commensurate with my intent and teaching, I would conduct an introspective review of the event to identify my own shortcomings, reflect on my rationale at the time, and attempt to lessen the impact by correcting and apologizing for the way I handled the situation. This personal after-action review and remediation can be painful, but it is crucial to building loyalty as a leader, to continuous self-improvement, and to forging a greater effort not to repeat the behavior. I have encouraged this type of review by those whom I have mentored, and it appears to have been instrumental in developing many of them to do the same.

I have made presentations of many aspects of this personal history and these lessons to leaders ranging from first-line military leaders and civilian supervisors to military senior commanders and civilian chief executive officers. Comments have been nearly universally positive, and several have recommended that I capture these lessons and how they came about into a permanent document to assist future evolving leaders. Many have also pointed out that most of these lessons fall into the category of common sense, but as the old adage points out, the use of common sense is not nearly as common as it should be.

Section 1: Early Life

My father was born in Meridian, Mississippi, and was raised in Highland Park in Dallas County, Texas. He was actively involved with the scouting program, becoming an Eagle Scout, and as a young adult, he was a scoutmaster. His love of the scouting program was lifelong, and he served as an adult leader or troop committee chairman for troops or packs for military families in the Free Territory of Trieste; Heidelberg, Germany; Fort Hood, Texas; and Keflavik, Iceland. He attended Virginia Military Institute until he was injured playing football, and he subsequently graduated from Southern Methodist University. He was commissioned in the U.S. Army Reserve (USAR) through the Reserve Officers' Training Corps program, and he entered active duty as an infantry officer in September, 1940, being initially assigned to the 9th Infantry Division (ID) at Fort Bragg, North Carolina.

My mother was born in Boston, Massachusetts, and was raised on Cape Cod in the town of Barnstable. My parents met at a social event while my father was on temporary duty at Camp Edwards on Cape Cod, where he was training for amphibious operations. They were married in August 1942 and settled briefly at Fort Bragg, but five months later moved to Camp Gordon Johnston in Carrabelle, Florida, where he was assigned as an instructor and then director of training, until he was reassigned to the Amphibious Training Center at Fort Pierce, Florida. At Fort Pierce, my father served as an instructor in amphibious operations and also served as a liaison officer to the Navy, serving aboard the USS *Manley* off the Atlantic coast and off the African and European coasts. He subsequently became the director of training over the Shore Party, Beach Party, Scout and Raider, Navy Demolition, Army Demolition, and DUKW Schools, and Small Boat and Engineer Board Training. As World War II was coming to an end, it was anticipated that there would have to be a major amphibious assault on Japan to bring the war in the Pacific to a conclusion, so it was thought that he would join the Army planning staff in the Pacific to lend his expertise to the operation. This, of course, was of grave concern to my mother, as by then she had two boys under the age of two. However, the decision to use atomic weapons obviated the need for an amphibious assault with tens if not hundreds of thousands of casualties. Instead, he served as director of training until May 1946, when he was reassigned to Korea to assume command of the 3rd Battalion (BN), 32nd Infantry Regiment based out of Chuncheon, Korea, just south of the 38th Parallel with the mission of operating a series of outposts monitoring the 38th Parallel, which served as the dividing line between North and South Korea following World War II.

Most tours in Korea were unaccompanied (meaning that no family members came along) and of thirteen months' duration. The country was still devastated from World War II, and the infrastructure was lacking. Tensions along the 38th Parallel were increasing between the South (supported by the United States) and the North (supported by the USSR). Water was not drinkable without treatment, and most local produce was contaminated. However, for unit stability, key leaders were expected to be there for twenty-four months, and dependents (family members) were authorized. Military housing for families was not yet developed in Chuncheon, and my mother was expecting another child in December, so rather than accompany my father at the time, we were settled on Cape Cod with my mother's family until we could join him in Korea the following year.

Our journey to Korea very much typifies the commitment, sacrifice, and strength of military spouses in that era. My grandparents dropped my mother off at the train station in Boston and she set off by herself with three boys, ages four, two and a half, and six months. We traveled by train from Boston to Chicago, where we had a scheduled layover of several hours so my father's mother could meet us and assist my mother in changing trains and provide her with a brief respite before we continued on. In San Francisco, we boarded the USAT *General R. M. Blatchford*, an Army troop transport ship, and sailed to Korea. This was particularly challenging for my mother, as troop ships provided little in the way of safety or convenience for children. My father met us at Inchon Harbor, and we traveled by Jeep up into the mountains to Chuncheon, in the foothills just below the 38th Parallel which divided North and South Korea. This journey took over a month to complete, and conveyances (cars, trains, and ships) were not air conditioned. In that era, instant formula did not exist, and most women in her peer group did not breast feed, as there were few, if any, accommodations to support this. Baby formula was prepared using evaporated milk and corn syrup; baby bottles were glass and had to be sterilized by boiling before each use; disposable diapers did not exist, so dirty diapers had to be hand washed and dried. (My mother used to dry them by holding them out the window of the train or automobile as we traveled.) For safety, my older brother and I were in harnesses and on leashes most of the time. On deck, she would often find another passenger or a soldier or sailor willing to hold a baby or a leash for a short time.

Life in Korea in the late 1940s was difficult, even though household help was plentiful and inexpensive. Officers were allowed to purchase surplus military Jeeps from World War II, and these served as our "privately owned vehicles." They were poorly heated and extremely crowded for a family of five. Winters were brutally cold, with a fair amount of snow. The Military Exchange (department store) and Commissary (grocery store) had a very limited selection, and mail-order items (mostly from the Sears catalog) took weeks to arrive. Virtually all water supplies required treatment by boiling or the addition of halazone tablets. With internet communications fifty years in the future and telephone service limited and expensive, letter writing was the primary means to stay in touch with family and friends, though it took at least a week each way for delivery. Very few families were allowed on each post, mostly officers and their wives. Nevertheless, my mother loved her time with my father and us under these conditions. She and my father developed lifelong friendships with the other families, though for the few children there, the age disparities and difficult communications limited such friendships. The South Korean people were incredibly friendly and had a genuine interest in the children. During my father's tour in Korea we were able to visit many beautiful and historic sites not seen by most Americans, and unfortunately not fully appreciated by us as very young children. One Korean youth who assisted my mother at the house later became an officer in the South Korean Army, and he remained in touch with my parents throughout their lives and visited them in the United States years later.

My father commanded a battalion with the mission of maintaining a series of outposts along the 38th Parallel. This, too, was a stressor for my mother, as this was not without risk. As he was at the end of a long logistics system, my father struggled with a personnel shortage and shortages of fuel, munitions, rations, and equipment. It was extremely frustrating to him (and I am sure the other commanders) not to be fully resourced, which made it extraordinarily difficult to maintain a high degree of readiness in the presence of a significant potential threat.

We returned to the United States in 1948 on another troop ship, the USAT *General A. W. Greely*. Conditions were essentially the same, and our cabin was more crowded with the addition of my father, but at least my younger brother was walking and my father was there to assist my mother with the three of us.

Arriving back in California, my parents bought a new 1949 Packard convertible, and we set out to drive to Washington DC for my father's next assignment. At that time in our nation's history, the interstate highway system did not exist and the majority of highways were only two lanes. According to my father, the Army allotted time for 300 miles per day when families were traveling by privately owned vehicles for official military moves. In addition, leave (vacation) time (referred to as "delay en route") was authorized for up to thirty days during a permanent change of station (PCS). As my mother had never visited the southwest, they took the opportunity to visit historic locations. I can still recall the Sequoia National Forest, Petrified Forest, and Grand Canyon, but I am sure there were other locations as well. What I do recall vividly was how unpleasant it was to travel by car for long distances. It was August and therefore extremely hot, particularly as we crossed the desert (and cars in those days did not have air conditioners). In the mornings, my mother would hold wet clothes washed in the sink or tub the night before out her window to dry. In the afternoon, my parents would place a metal box they had purchased in the passenger window to cool the car. It had slits in the sides and held a block of ice, over which air would flow. Both the drying clothes held out the front window by my mother in the morning and the flow from the air cooler in the afternoon drenched the three boys in the back seat, making the journey even more unpleasant for my brothers and me. Nevertheless, this was also the time of my first long-term memories of America. Our route took us to Dallas to visit my father's family and friends, and to relax and break up the long drive. From there we were off to Cape Cod to visit my mother's family with stops along the way to visit battlefields and Rock City Gardens in Tennessee (for years the favorite place of my brothers and me) and battlefields in Virginia and Pennsylvania. Finally, after six weeks on the road, we arrived in Arlington, Virginia, where we would live for the next three years. Other than the features mentioned, I cannot recall many details of this trip, but I do remember that compared to our limited travels in Korea, America seemed huge, seemed to go on forever, and was so different from place to place across the country.

My formative years began in DC. I began to get to know both of my parents' families. On my father's side, my grandfather passed away shortly before I was born, so there was only my grandmother, my uncle, and a few second cousins. My grandmother would visit occasionally, as would my uncle who was in the Navy Reserve. However, on my mother's side, both of my grandparents were still living on Cape Cod and my mother's sister lived in Chevy Chase, Maryland, with her family, so we saw them fairly frequently. We regularly visited Cape Cod during that period and in subsequent summers when we traveled into and out of the United Sates.

My father served in the Pentagon on the Army General Staff and had to travel a fair amount. However, life was relatively stable throughout this period, though my mother was often quite stressed when he went away. Later, I was to learn that a great source of her anxiety was that he was developing expertise in nuclear weapons and had traveled to Sandia Base, New Mexico, and Camp Desert Rock, Nevada, to train in the use of nuclear weapons. He had personally observed the effects of an atomic bomb detonation from a trench close to the explosion so that he could sense the flash and feel the overpressure blast and heat from the explosion. (There are a number of videos online which can be found by entering "Camp Desert Rock atomic explosions" into a search engine.) When I recalled this later in my career, I realized that this was the first example I observed of the impact of unanticipated and unintended consequences of events. Specifically, my father sought the nuclear weapons training to prepare for subsequent assignments in Europe, where the potential existed for the use of tactical nuclear weapons, but when the Korean War broke out, he very much desired as an infantry officer to command troops in battle; he had not had the opportunity to do so in World War II, and he was particularly well prepared from his service in Korea to do this. However, due to his knowledge of nuclear weapons, the Army leadership was unwilling to risk having him on the ground in Korea, where he might potentially become a prisoner of war. On the positive side, my mother really needed him at that time due to the anxiety provoked by an accident at Fort Leavenworth (discussed later), and the family clearly benefited by having him with us. Many years later, he told me that there was a belief among some that soldiers could be "hardened" to the effects of radiation. I know he observed at least one demonstration in a forward position, but I do not know if he observed more than that. The real negative consequences, though, were not apparent until years later when, as a physician, I realized that his early development of cataracts, heart disease, and declining health were undoubtedly due to the radiation exposure from his training.

Another unanticipated consequence came from my parents' decision for me to start the first grade a year early since I would not turn six until late December and normally would not have started the first grade until the following September. Academically, I was clearly ready and from our periods of relative isolation and home schooling by my mother, I could already read and do arithmetic above the first-grade level. However, as a result of the relative isolation of my father's assignments, I had not developed the physical ability or emotional capacity to interact well with my new peer group, in which I was the youngest and smallest. This came back to haunt me over the years, as we moved relatively frequently and I changed peer groups yearly. Consequently, I had the disadvantage of being the newest to the class, the youngest, the smallest, and also one of the most advanced academically. These are not characteristics that generally endear a boy to his peers, and they do not make for popularity in school. Early on I would attempt to compensate by fostering mischief, but my parents quickly squelched that behavior, or at least any open manifestations of it.

From early childhood, my brothers and I frequently wore miniature uniforms and clothing either purchased at the Post Exchange or made for us from material taken from my father's old uniforms. We had miniature soldiers, tanks, and artillery toys that "fought" battles on the floor. During this assignment, my father, who was a military historian, took us to a variety of battlefields in the vicinity of Washington and New England, and in subsequent assignments to battlefields in Italy, Germany, France, and Belgium. On these tours, he regaled us with tales of the dynamics of the particular battles and the valor demonstrated by American and British soldiers and leaders on both sides. I was most impressed by all of this, resulting in a conscious desire to become a soldier.

Following the tour in DC, we accompanied my father to Fort Leavenworth, Kansas, where he attended the Army Command and General Staff College (C&GSC) to prepare selected officers for higher-level assignments. My early memories of Fort Leavenworth focused on the good family time associated with the academic schedule of the institution, the proximity to Dallas, and the limited amount of travel for my father. My older brother and I got our first bicycles and learned to ride, and my older brother joined the Cub Scouts. However, later in this tour the young son of one of my father's classmates from Belgium—a close family friend—was killed when a milk truck backed over him in our small neighborhood. My mother became deeply depressed after this and changed in many ways. While she remained quite sociable with her circle of friends and still interacted well and continued her outgoing nature with adults, she became overanxious for our safety and very controlling, constantly keeping us in her sight and limiting our interaction with others. As a direct consequence of this event and my mother's reaction, my brothers and I gradually turned inward; although we had been quite outgoing before, my older brother and I became very introverted.

After the C&GSC, my father was assigned as the Assistant Chief of Staff for Plans and Operations for the Commanding General of the Army Forces for the Trust Territory of Trieste (TRUST). Normally, overseas movement of officers and families at that time was by Military Sea Transport. However, the need for my father in Trieste was sufficiently urgent to warrant movement by air, and we were given an Aerial Port of Call for Westover Air Force Base outside of Springfield, Massachusetts. This allowed us to go by privately owned vehicle (the Packard convertible) to the East Coast, ship the car to Trieste, visit my grandparents on Cape Cod, and report to Westover AFB for travel. We had to arrive at the airfield at 4:00 a.m. and were taken out to the aircraft, an unpressurized four-propeller converted tanker with troop seats along the sides and litters in the front and cargo in the rear. Our first stop was at Lajes Field in the Azores, where we would refuel. Since my father was a senior officer, there was a greeting party for him and a vehicle to take us to the terminal. The landing was quite turbulent; upon landing my younger brother turned toward my father and vomited on his dress uniform. Not to be outdone, I did the same shortly thereafter from the other side. This made for an awkward formal greeting for my father, though he took it in stride. While the aircraft was refueling they quickly arranged for him to get cleaned up and even had his uniform cleaned before we re-boarded the aircraft for the next leg of the journey to Wheelus Air Base in Tripoli, Libya.

Libya was supposed to be a short layover before heading to Athens, but the aircraft broke down and parts had to be sent for from the United States, resulting in a one-week stay. We were billeted in a hotel with openings for windows but no glass or screens and a large ceiling fan for cooling. We were by the shore, but a ship had just purged its bilges off the coast and the water was badly contaminated and closed for swimming or even wading. We had time and opportunity for sightseeing and were fascinated by the bazaars and the camels along the streets, as well as the combination of exotic and noxious smells. Of particular interest was the castle on the bay which we could see across the waterfront.

From Libya, we traveled to Athens, Greece, with a brief delay which allowed for touring the historic sites and then on to Rome, where we also had a couple of days to be tourists. From there we traveled by train to Trieste. (My father later commented that, ironically, we might have gotten there sooner by ship, but it was a great sightseeing tour.)

At first, the time in Trieste was ideal. My mother gave birth to my sister the following July, and we attended school regularly. Although my mother was still overprotective, this was a significant distraction, and my brothers and I enjoyed a bit greater freedom of movement. I joined my older brother in the Cub Scouts, and my father served as the chairman of the pack committee. The Italian people were friendly, and we had family friends from both our time in Korea and Fort Leavenworth stationed here. My mother was back in her comfort zone with an active social life as an officer's wife. We lived in a nice duplex in a small cluster of military-leased housing on the side of a mountain overlooking Trieste. Less than half a mile above our house were the ruins of a castle, and with our new freedom of action, my brothers and I and our new friends would slip away, climb the hill, crawl under the fence, and explore the ruins. Neither the police nor our parents found out, so we avoided the natural consequences of our actions.

For my parents, there were the usual inconveniences of a relatively remote assignment. Tap water was not yet drinkable, fresh milk was not available, and shopping was from a limited selection for food (Commissary) and personal items (Post Exchange) or by catalog from the United

States, which would take weeks. Our one car had a failure of the closing mechanism for the left rear window, and it took over a month for the part. (Instead of fighting over who had to sit in the center seat, we fought over who had to be by the open window.) Our house overlooked the city and the bay, and my father's office was in the Miramare Castle on the Adriatic. The military hospital was away from the housing area, and to go from our house to my father's office, the medical facility, or the dependents school we had to go through the central plaza of the city. This was fascinating the first year, watching the Italians in the market places, but became quite problematic as tensions increased between the Italians and the Yugoslavians over the future of Trieste. By the start of school in 1953, classes were frequently suspended due to the risk profile of the community on a day-by-day basis, and, on the days that we had school, the school bus, which had to travel through the center of town, required extra security from armed military police. Security was heightened across the board, which only increased the anxiety of my parents, particularly my mother, and proved limiting for us children. By early November all families were evacuated from Trieste. We were moved to a hotel in Viareggio on the Tyrrhenian Sea while my father remained in Trieste until the end of November.

These were once again stressful times for my mother. She was in a foreign country, with other families in the same position, with limited support from the military and with limited Italian language skills. She had three boys, ages ten, seven, and five, but also a four-month-old daughter. Even though my father was only across Italy, communication with him was limited, and she was concerned for his safety. Fortunately, this did not last long and my father received instructions in just under a month to relocate the family to Berchtesgaden, Germany, and remain there, awaiting his next assignment and onward movement orders. We set off from Viareggio in the 1949 Packard convertible with a homemade plywood roof rack fabricated by soldiers working with my father. My parents had to place the majority of our household goods in storage pending further movement orders when we departed Trieste, so we had only those essential items, including clothing, that we would need for a period of one to two months or longer and which would fit in the trunk or on the roof of the car. My sister was in the front with my mother and father, and the three boys were in the back. My parents arranged for German friends to take our family dog, a standard poodle, and deliver him to us once we were settled somewhere in Western Europe, most likely Germany, as there was absolutely no room for him in the car. We arrived in Berchtesgaden in early December and checked into the Berchtesgadener Hof Hotel, a former historic Third Reich hotel that had been taken over by the U.S. military.

We were not familiar with German customs and traditions yet, but we knew that the Christmas season was just beginning. We were told that on the evening of December 5, Krampus would be coming to see the little children and we all erroneously assumed it was a jovial figure, perhaps a German Santa Claus. That evening, all of the evacuee children were crowded into the front hall when the door burst open and this horrific figure dressed in black came in shouting at the children and whacking those he could reach with a handful of switches. This is exactly what a group of evacuee children—already traumatized by the stressful situation in Trieste, the disruption of the school year, the fathers remaining in Trieste, and the sudden move—did not need! The memories of that night are still vivid after sixty-five years. Many years later, my wife, Ann, and I were stationed in Germany for eight years with only an eleven-month break for a military school in Carlisle, Pennsylvania. Living there for so many years with family and close friends, we adopted many German traditions including advent calendars for the first twenty-five days of December, which included a small piece of chocolate behind the number for each day. We also recognized Saint Nicholas Day, when the children would leave their shoes out the night before and they would find candy and small gifts in them the morning of December 6. However, the Krampus is forever banned from our home!

After Christmas, my father received his orders for Heidelberg, and we lived there for eighteen months—or one half and then one full school year. We lived in German housing seized after World War II in a small neighborhood with other senior Army officers and fewer than ten families, remote from the primary military housing areas. Although this continued our life of relative isolation, I was pleasantly surprised years later to find that three of the other children from that small group were at West Point the same time as I was. Even in peacetime, the standard tour in the Army was three years, which for children means that when you arrive, one-third of the kids you meet will be gone in a year, one-third will be settled and may take on a few new friends, and one-third are new like you. It is rare under these conditions to find and develop lifelong friends. For my family, the only two times while growing up that we had the luxury of a three-year tour were in Washington DC and Fayetteville, Arkansas, although in both of these assignments, we were not in military family housing or the dependents schools, so we effectively were the new kids for all three years.

My memories of this period primarily include the many trips we took, visiting Belgium, Holland, France, and areas within the U.S. Zone of Germany. We saw many castles, as well as ruins from World War II. The biggest impression was the horrible impact of war and the massive devastation that can be wrought on a person's home country. Not wanting to see this happen in America was clearly a factor inducing all three of us boys to enter the Army ourselves and be willing to serve in combat assignments in foreign lands.

Nevertheless, by then, several areas in West Germany were well on their way to recovery, and the industrious nature of the German people was obvious. On the amusing side, every road seemed to lead to a place called *Umleitung*, which my parents told us was a special part of every town in Germany. Later, we learned in German class that this was actually the word for detour and reflected the major reconstruction underway. This was a relatively stable time for the family, although there was a monthly alert, usually at 2:00 a.m., and we always had to have a case of C rations and other supplies in the trunk of the car in case the threat of war became high enough for the Noncombatant Evacuation Order to be issued, in which case families would have to travel to assigned locations to assemble for evacuation from the area at risk and ultimately back to the United States.

My older brother had started in a scouting program at Fort Leavenworth, and my younger brother and I each joined as soon as we were eligible. Scouting served as a stabilizing force for the family, as programs were in place at every military installation. The programs played a major role in our lives as we progressed in Cub Scouts and Boy Scouts. My parents were very supportive of the program, and my father held an adult leadership role in each of these programs. He took great pride in our participation and successes, with all three boys becoming Eagle Scouts. The values in the Boy Scouts of America became a critical component of our family values and brought us closer together. Specifically, Scouting helped instill in us three major duties in life—duty to God, duty to country, and duty to self. The elements of the Scout Law, "A Scout is Trustworthy, Loyal, Helpful, Friendly, Courteous, Kind, Obedient, Cheerful, Thrifty, Brave, Clean, and Reverent," instilled in us by both the program and our parents served as the base of our foundation. Even today, at age seventy-four, these words play a role when I make key decisions in life.

My father's next assignment was to Fort Hood, Texas. This time there was no urgency for him to arrive, so we returned by ship, the normal means of travel in that era. Our parents sold the old Packard and ordered a Ford station wagon to be picked up upon arrival in New York. Our port of call was out of Bremerhaven for the USNS *General Maurice Rose*, a larger and faster class of military transport ships than the *Blatchford* and *Greely* that had carried us between San Francisco and Korea. Based on family size (and my father's seniority) we were allocated two cabins, giving us a bit more space. Although there was no comparison to a commercial ocean liner, there were a few amenities, including a small movie theater on board and an area where pets were allowed, so we were able to bring along our dog. There was a space behind the bridge where the animals were crated, and owners could walk their pets as long as they cleaned up behind them.

After we arrived in New York, we picked up our new car (which did not seem much more spacious than when we left Trieste in the Packard convertible, given our growth and the addition of the dog). We visited my mother's family on Cape Cod, then headed to Dallas to visit my grandmother and uncle, and finally to Fort Hood. This was during the initial construction of the interstate highway system, so most of the travel was still on two-lane roads through multiple small towns. The first year there was great from my perspective. Fort Hood is the home of the III Corps and has always had at least one Armor Division stationed there. There is constant training being held, and my father would take us out to observe whenever possible. I attended Meadows Elementary School on the post, and even had the opportunity to make some friends who were new arrivals with us. Scouting was a high point, with camping on Belton Lake and the surrounding area. We traveled to Waco to participate in a Scout Fair, at which our troop built a twenty-foot tower from previously cut logs using rope lashings. Our house backed up to the golf course, and

I would watch the golfers, sell back lost balls, and long to learn to play, but time and finances interfered, much to my long-term regret. My early propensity for mischief surfaced briefly when a group of us started ambushing arriving buses with mud balls, but this was terminated when the Military Police caught the group of us. Our group consisted of the sons of two generals and four colonels, and the Provost Marshal chose to call our mothers and let them tell our fathers, which ended the ambushes.

All was well until the autumn of 1956 when I entered Rancier Junior High School in Killeen, Texas. The military children going from sixth to seventh grade were split up among existing peer groups, again making us the new kids. I never had more than one person I already knew in any of my classes or home room. This was a great awakening for me, as (in my opinion) the school was run like a prison. For the most part, gone were the friendly and caring Department of Defense dependents school teachers who I thought had a genuine interest in our development, to be replaced by teachers that I considered for the most part to be tyrants who primarily enforced discipline with corporal punishment. As with any rule, there was an exception: Mrs. Joyce, who had been my brother's home room teacher the previous year, helped salvage the year for me when I was floundering under a particularly tyrannical teacher by arranging for me to transfer to her class. The most vivid impression this school made on me came early in my time there. I was standing in line for the water fountain when another boy pushed me out of line. A teacher passing by saw me out of line and whacked me with a paddle that was about a half inch thick, about eighteen inches long, and with holes drilled through it to make it go faster and inflict more pain, and sent me to the back of the line without even bothering to find out what happened. This pattern was pervasive and never would have been allowed in a Department of Defense school or any school in the United States today. Having lived in Korea and Europe, I was not impressed with the value of Texas history and Texas geography, which also did not help. I must confess that by the time we left Fort Hood and despite my father's family being from Dallas, I had a degree of appreciation for the sentiment attributed to General Sheridan that if he owned Hell and he owned Texas, he would rent out Texas and live in Hell. Fortunately, my two strongest subjects were mathematics and English, so I got by, but I was not at all upset when our projected three-year tour was curtailed to seventeen months and we were off to Keflavik, Iceland, well before the end of the school year.

Every permanent change of station for my father meant a road trip and a visit to Cape Cod, and this was no exception. Although it was great to visit family, for my brothers and me, Cape Cod in April and early May was not like visiting in July and August. This time our aerial port of call was through McGuire Air Force Base outside Philadelphia. We flew in a Military Air Transport Service C-118, which was a big step up from our previous flight to Europe, as this aircraft also had four propellers, but was pressurized, with real airplane seats, and windows. We flew to Gander, Newfoundland, and had a brief break while the plane was refueled and serviced. As we continued to the northeast, we could see icebergs in the ocean and we could tell that the days were getting longer. Since my father was assigned as the Commander, Army Forces Iceland, there was a formal welcome ceremony for him at the airfield, and I have to acknowledge the pride we felt in the honors bestowed on our father. I was also awed by the Navy and Air Force surveillance and combat aircraft at the base. My father was even able to arrange for our family dog to join us in Iceland. (I'm not sure how many rules or laws my father and his Air Force friends broke in accomplishing this. Dogs were only allowed to be imported to Iceland from England due to concern for rabies, so my father had arranged with friends in the Air Force to fly the dog from New Jersey to England and avoid the U.K. quarantine by changing planes on the airfield tarmac for a plane bound for the NATO Base at Keflavik.)

Living in Iceland was a grand adventure. An annual high mark for the service members and families stationed there was the July 4th baseball game played outdoors without artificial lights. We rapidly became involved in the Boy Scouts and participated in many activities, including visiting thermal areas and geysers, hiking on glaciers, and camping with the Icelandic Scouts (Boy Scouts and Girl Scouts in the same camps). We were flown over the Arctic Circle in an Air Force C 47 ("Gooney Bird"), a twin-engine World War II aircraft, and we attended summer camp in England near Sheffield Forest with the Air Force providing transportation. We took full advantage of the long days and midnight sun. Winters were also fun in many ways. Because of the location in the north Atlantic, temperatures were relatively mild but the wind was almost always strong. We were issued parkas by the Air Force that had a base identification badge on the front and a red reflector in the back. The wind could cause significant snow drifts, wide but not so high as to be dangerous, so we made snow caves, tunnels, and forts. When there was ice on the street, we would open up our parkas to form a sail and let the wind blow us down the street.

I earned the Swimming and Life Saving Merit Badges at an indoor pool in Reykjavik and became an Eagle Scout at age thirteen. My leadership development began as a Patrol Leader of eight Scouts, followed by six months as Senior Patrol Leader for the troop. My first lessons in leadership were the need for preparation, the need to listen, and the difficulty in leading peers with differing ideas and viewpoints. This was where I first discovered that influence trumps authority, as a Boy Scout Patrol Leader has no authority and, barring violence which was prohibited, the leader must learn to use influence and consensus building to be successful.

There was only one television channel: Armed Forces Radio and Television. It came on at 6:00 p.m. and went off at midnight. Children's shows were early, followed by news and programs for teens and adults. If you missed your favorite show, there were no recording options, so we were all sensitive to the time.

These were great years for my mother, perhaps her best. She thrived in the role of a senior commander's wife, providing support and mentoring to the young officers' wives. She also enjoyed the international aspects of the command and the interaction with diplomats and leading Icelandic officials and their wives. In addition, she enjoyed our many trips exploring the country, visiting grottos on the ocean, inland glaciers, beautiful waterfalls, and ancient lava fields. I think it was here that she finally let go of the gloom from the death of the child at Fort Leavenworth.

Schooling was problematic for older dependent children. The Department of Defense school in Iceland only went through the eighth grade (where my class had about twelve children). For high school (9–12) there was the option of boarding school in Frankfurt, Germany, or remaining in Iceland with our families, where we had a single classroom in a Quonset hut, fewer than thirty students total for grades 9–12, and a proctor who monitored our work on correspondence courses from the University of Maryland and also monitored any required testing. We did not have a teacher, only a proctor who could offer limited advice on selecting classes. We worked at our own direction and pace. Hence, there were frequent issues for those of us remaining in Iceland with our parents in terms of placement upon return to America. After my experience in Texas, I hated history and I loved mathematics, so I took two years of mathematics and zero years of history in the ninth grade. There were not any school or community youth sports or other activities except Little League baseball, youth basketball, and scouting. There were no high school sports at all. Many families would send their children back to their families in the United States or to the Department of Defense school in Frankfurt, which provided a boarding school option, reducing the number of high school–aged students on base. Other service members would opt for a one-year unaccompanied tour, leaving their families in the United States. This caused a sense of isolation among those of us remaining with our parents.

After two years, it was time to move again. For me, this would be my ninth move and I was not yet fifteen years old. A major portion of my life to this point had been outside of the United States, but this was to change. My father was reassigned to Fayetteville, Arkansas, as a professor of military science at the University of Arkansas.

The trip to Fayetteville was much the reverse of our trip to Iceland. From Keflavik, we flew on a C 118 to Gander for a stopover and refueling. However, shortly after takeoff on the flight to McGuire, we could see oil streaming from the inboard engine on the right side of the plane. Shortly thereafter, the propeller stopped and we spent the next hour circling Gander looking at the ice in the water and the fuel streaming out as the plane jettisoned most of the fuel to decrease the risk of fire upon landing. This all turned out to be anxiety provoking but unremarkable, except the plane could not be repaired quickly, so we had to return to the terminal and await a replacement aircraft. The pilot was a friend of my father who had flown the airplane up to Keflavik specifically to bring us back to America, but he had to stay with the plane so we had dinner with his family the next night while his good deed did not go unpunished.

From there it was a slightly different route to Fayetteville, entering Arkansas from Missouri and cutting across the northern part of the state. We rented a house at 311 East Prospect Street, and then went on to Dallas to visit my grandmother and to wait for our household goods to arrive from Iceland so we could move in.

My time in Fayetteville turned out to be a defining period of my life. As is evident from this narrative, we had previously never lived anywhere long enough to engender a sense of belonging. In many ways, we felt like we were military nomads, though perhaps a better term would be *generic Americans*. It is true that we could have said that we were from Dallas or Cape Cod, but we only visited family in these locations. Whether we lived in the United States or abroad, we really did not know the community beyond the military and were ignorant of the environment, the local culture, and often even the language. This is insufficient for a sense of belonging. However, we were raised with a strong sense of pride in being Americans and a love for a country that we hardly knew. My parents always insisted that as a family overseas, we served as ambassadors for our country and must constantly behave as such. They instilled in us a strong sense of loyalty to America and a high value set. As we were very active in the Boy Scouts of America, we had multiple opportunities to engage with Scouts from other countries. As both of my brothers and I were Eagle Scouts, we were instilled with a high sense of duty, particularly to God and country, and we developed a strong sense of honor and integrity. Nevertheless, until we moved to Fayetteville, we did not really belong anywhere in particular.

Taking correspondence courses for the ninth grade for me and ninth and tenth for my brother, focusing on courses at our own direction, left us way out of synch for a normal high school experience, so my parents chose to enroll us in the University High School in Peabody Hall on the University of Arkansas campus. There, Mr. Paul Eddy, another great mentor to many, was willing to work with us to complete our studies on time, if not in the proper order. We were ahead in some areas and behind in others, and he allowed us the flexibility to take higher-grade classes simultaneously with our current-grade classes and a couple of mandatory lower-grade classes that neither of us had taken (bothered with) in Iceland. As an example, I had to take Junior and Senior English simultaneously and ran out of mathematics courses before my senior year. The academic program, though limited in diversity of subjects, was ideal, as we had a combination of permanent faculty from the university and student teachers for all of our classes. Student teachers and faculty both would go out of their way to assist students and promote learning. A great example of this came when, in October of my senior year, I was caught reading a comic book in the back of the accounting class which I took because I had already finished all of the mathematics courses. The student teacher, when she questioned me, discovered that I really enjoyed the course and had already finished the text and had done all of the problems in the book. She allowed me to continue reading the comic book, but she showed up the next day with the college freshman text for me and placed me on an individual learning program.

Unfortunately, there were a couple of aspects which in retrospect were problematic. The first was my limited exposure to the vast variety of individual and team sports, although, despite having never played basketball (the only sport at the school) before, I was able to play on the junior varsity team. I did not realize what I was missing until later in life. The second was the limited exposure to others my age. My class had only twenty-two students, which was only slightly more than what I had in Keflavik, Iceland; I was still the youngest; and I was taking classes out of sequence. This reinforced my tendency to be an introvert and feel uncomfortable with large groups, a limiting factor which I fought to overcome through my entire adult life. It fell upon my friend Jimmy Highfill to draw me out.

Another important aspect of our lives is that we were raised as *generic Christians* as well. We were baptized into the Anglican or Episcopal Church, said our prayers at night with our parents, and attended church on a regular basis. However, the church that we attended varied based upon where we were and what military chaplains or civilian ministers or priests were available. I know that we at one time or another attended Catholic, Lutheran, Congregational, Methodist, Baptist, and general Protestant church services. We had a sound Christian religious foundation but no specific affiliation. Finally, in Fayetteville, we belonged to Saint Paul's Episcopal Church. We attended those services, and I joined the youth group, underwent Confirmation, and served as an Acolyte. Nevertheless, my sister, being many years younger, instead attended the Catholic school, and she and my mother were involved in much of their activities as well.

Fayetteville was (and still is) a great place to live. There is a vibrant academic community and a great collegiate athletic program for all sports, but particularly football and basketball as well as track and cross country. I saw my first football game and was amazed by the enthusiasm and the success of the Razorbacks under Coach Frank Broyles. I joined a Boy Scout troop and became the junior assistant scoutmaster. There were great places to camp in the area along the river in nearby Eureka Springs, both as a scout and with friends from high school.

Perhaps the most meaningful thing for me was that when I attended the University High School, I met Jim Highfill. He became my first real close friend outside of the family and was my first "best friend." Unfortunately, without the benefits of the social media tools of today, we lost touch with each other after high school, as I ended up with an Army career and he had a great career in the Navy. We actually were in Saudi Arabia for Operation Desert Storm at the same time, but neither of us was aware of that and we did not see each other again until 2010, when I returned to Arkansas and arranged a visit to Fayetteville to see him.

I had been raised to be a soldier someday and from my time in Iceland on, I wanted to attend West Point. However, in Fayetteville, I also felt a calling to the Anglican priesthood, which strengthened over the next four years, as I felt a strong sense of belonging and an increasing desire to serve. Simultaneously, my interest in being an Army officer increased as my brother Linwood III (Buddy) and I participated in the Reserve Officers' Training Corps at the University of Arkansas. Ultimately, I decided to apply for the Military Academy in the belief that if God wanted me to be a soldier, my application to West Point would be accepted, and if not, I would assume I was meant to be a priest and would orient my future toward seminary and the priesthood.

When I received my appointment to West Point, I accepted and committed myself to complete the education and training that would follow. Buddy continued at the University of Arkansas and was commissioned in the Army Chemical Corps. He served a tour in Vietnam with the 1st Infantry Division until he was severely injured and evacuated to Japan and then to the United States. He continued to serve on the faculty of the Chemical School at Fort McClellan, and we were together when I was stationed there. Later he served with the 3rd Infantry Division in Germany. There, he met and married Elfriede, who was a German citizen, and he left the Army to become a math and science teacher in the Department of Defense Dependents School (DoDDS) system. He died in 2006. Buddy never forgot our Fayetteville roots, and whenever he would design word problems for study and tests, he would use the names of our close friends in Fayetteville. At my 50th class reunion I shared this with our friends, who remembered him fondly.

The values instilled in me by my parents and the military leaders I was exposed to in my youth fit very well with the Army Values (defined later). However, in retrospect, there were a couple of flaws in my foundation. I was definitely introverted and introspective, I had difficulty with interpersonal relationships and making friends, and, while I met admission standards, I was not adept at any particular sport and was not as physically fit as I had to become. The fitness gap was closed while at West Point, and the other gaps were corrected early in my career as an Infantry Officer.

Captain Linwood Griffin Jr. and wife, Zelda Griffin, at Fort Bragg, North Carolina; 1942.

Newly constructed family housing (quarters) in Chuncheon in spring 1947. The center house with the Jeep in front is for the commander and family.

Griffin family at home in Korea in fall 1947. Left to right: Linwood III, Jack, Zelda, Robert, and Linwood Jr.

Zelda Griffin with sons Linwood (left) and Robert in family Jeep on highway near the 38th Parallel.

Families and friends gather at Inchon Port on June 27, 1948, to say farewell or board the troop ship, USAT A. W. Greely. Zelda is in the center, holding the blanket, with the boys.

Zelda is at the family's lifeboat station on the USAT Greely, with (left to right) Linwood III, Jack, and Robert; June 28, 1948.

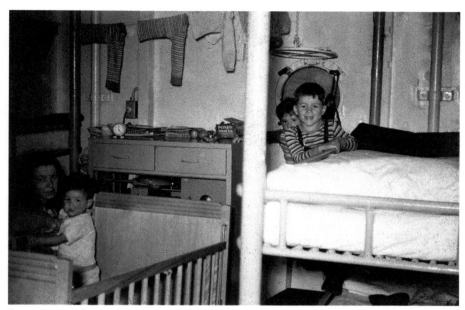

Somewhere on the Pacific Ocean, Zelda is in the family cabin on the USAT Greely with (left to right) Jack, Robert, and Linwood III. This cabin is essentially identical to the one she had on the USAT General R. M. Blatchford by herself with the three boys the year before.

Linwood III (center) with Jack (left) and Robert (right) on the deck of the USAT Greely.

Grandmother Beatrice Amanda Griffin in Arlington, Virginia (DC area), to help Zelda with Robert (right) and Jack (in lap) with chicken pox courtesy of Linwood III (left), who had nearly recovered.

Robert, Jack, and Linwood III in front of family quarters in "Pershing Park" at Fort Leavenworth; February 1951. Note: Robert's clothing is made from cut-down parts of military uniforms.

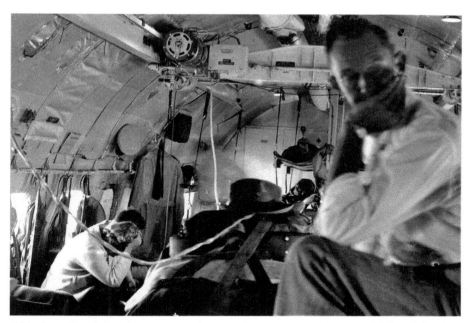

Zelda (seated) and three boys resting on litters at front en route to Azores and Libya; July 1951. Aircraft is a C-54, a four-engine propeller-driven, unpressurized airplane that transported the family from Westover AFB in Springfield, Massachusetts, to the Azores and on to Libya, 1952.

Zelda in front of Transient Quarters for a one-week stay in Tripoli; early August 1951.

The boys were fascinated with the castle on the bay in Tripoli seen in center of the photo; August 1952.

Cub Scout ceremony in the Free Territory of Trieste; January 1953. Linwood Griffin Jr. is on the far right with sons Linwood III and Robert.

The family lived in German housing in Heidelberg. Left to right: Robert, Linwood III, Zelda, Sherry (born in Trieste), and Jack.

Zelda with Sherry and Linwood III in family cabin on the USNS General Maurice Rose; *summer 1955.*

Linwood III (left) and Robert salute the colors at Fort Hood, Texas, in 1956.

In late summer 1957, the American Boy Scouts in Iceland were flown up over the Arctic Circle in a C-47 (two-engine propeller aircraft). Linwood III is second from left. Robert was across the aisle and is not shown.

American and Icelandic Boy Scouts crossing glacial runoff stream on a hike together; July 1958.

The Icelandic and American Boy Scouts take a break on their hike to a glacier together.

Campfire with American Boy Scouts and Icelandic Girl and Boy Scouts; 1958.

The entire eighth-grade class in Keflavik, Iceland, approaching graduation; May 1958. Robert is the third boy from the left. A Quonset hut serves as a classroom.

Robert (far left) and Jack (back row, third from right) with their new Boy Scout troop in Fayetteville, Arkansas; 1961.

Boys at Prairie Grove battlefield (left to right) Jack, Linwood III, and Robert.

Family portrait in Fayetteville, Arkansas, prior to Linwood Jr. departing to Korea for a year; 1962. Left to right: Linwood III, Jack, Zelda, Sherry, Linwood Jr., and Robert.

Saint Paul's Episcopal Church in Fayetteville, Arkansas, where Robert became seriously interested in a life serving as a priest rather than in the Army.

Zelda and Sherry at a Scout event with (left to right) Linwood III, Jack, and Robert—all Eagle Scouts.

Section 2: Military Service

Shortly before I arrived at West Point, General Douglas MacArthur made his farewell speech to the Corps of Cadets. This was recorded and played back to us on many occasions over the next four years. I was particularly touched by his introduction:

> Duty, Honor, Country. Those three hallowed words reverently dictate what you ought to be, what you can be, what you will be. They are your rallying points: to build courage when courage seems to fail; to regain faith when there seems to be little cause for faith; to create hope when hope becomes forlorn....They give you a temperate will, a quality of imagination, a vigor of the emotions, a freshness of the deep springs of life, a temperamental predominance of courage over timidity, an appetite for adventure over love of ease. They create in your heart the sense of wonder, the unfailing hope of what's next, and the joy and inspiration of life. They teach you in this way to be an officer...

During my career, both in and out of the Army, I have often recalled and been driven by his words and have drawn strength from them, particularly during my combat assignments in Vietnam and Saudi Arabia.

As mental training and career orientation, we were required to memorize a multitude of documents during our first two months at West Point. This was part of what is now called Cadet Basic Training, but in those days it was called "Beast Barracks." Three of these were particularly meaningful to me, and I carried them with me through my military and civilian careers. These were "Battalion Orders" by Brevet Major William Jenkins Worth (circa 1820), Major General John Schofield's Definition of Discipline (1879), and the West Point Cadet Prayer (circa 1924). The first of these sets the need for impartiality and consistency, the second focuses on the essential need to respect those you lead if you must count on them for success, and the third sets the stage and reinforces what General MacArthur, in 1963, told us we must be. I have shared these words with the men and women I have had the privilege to lead, and they are stated below with modifications by me in parentheses for civilian use. Although written for men, these words are relevant today to everyone.

But an officer (a leader) on duty knows no one—to be partial is to dishonor both himself and the object of his ill-advised favor. What will be thought of him who exacts of his friends that which disgraces him? Look at him who winks at and overlooks offences in one, which he causes to be punished in another, and contrast him with the inflexible soldier (leader) who does his duty faithfully, notwithstanding it occasionally wars with his private feelings. The conduct of one will be venerated and emulated, the other detested as a satire upon soldiership (leadership) and honor.

—Brevet Major William Jenkins Worth, circa 1820

The discipline which makes the soldiers (people) of a free country reliable in battle (business) is not to be gained by harsh or tyrannical treatment. On the contrary, such treatment is far more likely to destroy than to make an army (organization). It is possible to impart instruction and to give commands (direction) in such manner and such a tone of voice to inspire in the soldier (recipient) no feeling but an intense desire to obey, while the opposite manner and tone of voice cannot fail to excite strong resentment and a desire to disobey. The one mode or the other of dealing with subordinates (those you lead) springs from a corresponding spirit in the breast of the commander. He who feels the respect which is due to others cannot fail to inspire in them regard for himself, while he who feels, and hence manifests disrespect toward others, especially his inferiors, cannot fail to inspire hatred against himself.

—Major General John M. Schofield, August 11, 1879

O God, our Father, Thou Searcher of human hearts, help us to draw near to Thee in sincerity and truth. May our religion be filled with gladness and may our worship of Thee be natural.

Strengthen and increase our admiration for honest dealing and clean thinking, and suffer not our hatred of hypocrisy and pretense ever to diminish. Encourage us in our endeavor to live above the common level of life. Make us to choose the harder right instead of the easier wrong, and never to be content with a half-truth when the whole can be won. Endow us with courage that is born of loyalty to all that is noble and worthy, that scorns to compromise with vice and injustice and knows no fear when truth and right are in jeopardy. Guard us against flippancy and irreverence in the sacred things of life. Grant us new ties of friendship and new opportunities of service. Kindle our hearts in fellowship with those of a cheerful countenance, and soften our hearts with sympathy for those who sorrow and suffer. Help us to maintain the honor of the Corps untarnished and unsullied and to show forth in our lives the ideals of West Point in doing our duty to Thee and to our Country. All of which we ask in the name of the Great Friend and Master of all.

—Chaplain (Colonel) Clayton E. Wheat, circa 1924

I did not enjoy my time at West Point, though the education was outstanding. I felt that too much of the leadership demonstrated in that era was abysmal and reflected the norms of an earlier time. As new cadets, we were required to memorize elements from military history such as General Schofield's Definition of Discipline and Worth's Battalion Orders while simultaneously we were subjected to the hypocrisy (contrary to the tenets of the Cadet Prayer) on display from the first day. Orders were shouted by upperclassmen with their faces three inches from the new cadets, and the orders were not subject to questions if not understood. Although prohibited, physical and mental hazing were still deliberately overlooked by the leadership. Punishment was swift and excessive for even minor transgressions. Even some of the academic programs were excessively rigid and inflexible. What probably annoyed me the most in the first year's academics was solving a mathematics problem in a mathematically correct manner, but then being punished for not having used the "approved" solution. In first-year English, I had ranked near the top of the class early in the year but had the same instructor over multiple section changes, only to have him comment on an English paper that I was fortuitously and unconsciously choosing words that demonstrated insights beyond my capacity. Fortunately, for the final examination, I was with a different instructor and obtained the maximum score possible for my essay. I frequently considered leaving the Academy and continuing my academic studies elsewhere, but having committed myself to the Academy, I was too stubborn to abandon my chosen path. That noted, the biggest positive from my perspective was that exposure to this negative leadership sparked my lifelong desire to capture lessons on both how to lead in a manner that causes others to want to follow you and how to recognize actions that must be avoided to maintain the respect needed to lead others.

Despite my less-than-fond memories of my time at West Point, I have remained in contact with the Academy and several of my classmates, and I have been rewarded by watching the constant improvement and modernization of the institution. Having visited the U.S. Military Academy twice within the past year to participate in a leadership seminar and attend the fiftieth reunion of my class, I am pleased to have concluded that cadets at all levels are treated by the vast majority of their fellow cadets and the officers in a professional military manner; they are absolutely expected to treat each other the same way, and most do so. Consideration for others is considered a key component of leadership at the Academy and thereafter, whether in or out of the military. I can easily recommend the Military Academy to young men and women of today as a strong academic institution committed to the development of leaders of character.

Upon graduation from the U.S. Military Academy, I was commissioned as a Second Lieutenant of Infantry. This was followed by the Infantry Officers Basic Course (IOBC) and Ranger training at Fort Benning, Georgia. My background as a youth and my education at West Point left me fully endowed with the U.S. Army Values, which have served me well ever since:

Loyalty/Duty/Respect
Selfless Service/Honor/Integrity
Personal Courage

IOBC was primarily a technical course. It covered the essentials of the Infantry Branch—that is, how to "close with" (move through enemy fire to engage in direct combat with rifles, pistols, bayonets, or knives) and destroy the enemy. We covered movement to contact, combat assaults, security of the objective, preparing for a counter attack, identifying defensive fields of fire, use and emplacement of weapons systems (positioning weapons but also checking for avenues of approach, selecting the most advantageous position, and marking fields of fire with aiming stakes), and similar essentials of combat operations as an infantryman. Two important concepts which I did not realize until much later had civilian relevance as well were "prepping the battlefield" and "lane train-ing." These will be elaborated further in Section 3.

Ranger training is the Army's premier leadership training program for officers and noncommissioned officers. It is highly selective and phys-ically and mentally challenging. Fewer than half graduate and receive the "Ranger" certification uniform tab in a single attempt. We learned and were evaluated on techniques of patrolling, and we demonstrated leadership of small-unit operations over a two-month period involving woodland, mountain, and swamp operations with scarce rations, little sleep, and no regard for weather conditions. I learned to lead no matter how tired, hungry, cold, wet, or miserable I may be. We rotated leader-ship roles, but when tested as a leader, to succeed, each leader had to demonstrate attention to the needs of the soldiers on the team as well as accomplish the mission. This particular point came home to me during an operation in the swamps of Florida when we were ten days into a patrol with no more than one C-ration meal daily, four hours sleep per night, rain, and an ambient temperature in the mid-30s. I was the pla-toon leader, and four of my former West Point classmates were the squad leaders. As we moved through the swampy terrain, I realized that they were not maintaining discipline within their squads. Specifically, they were not making sure that their teams were constantly vigilant for the aggressor force and that all potential fields of fire were covered. I halted the platoon and called my squad leaders back. I told them that I was convinced that we were all failing in our responsibilities as leaders and that they had five minutes to get their soldiers back on the ball and move out smartly or I was going to relieve them of their positions before the Ranger cadre relieved us all. Later, reflecting back to Worth's Battalion Orders caused me to realize that I would enforce standards even for my own brother if he failed to do the right thing and I was responsible and accountable for his actions. It also was a reminder that discipline is both a noun referring to consistently doing the right thing and a verb in using punitive measures, if necessary, to get that point across. In the after-ac-tion review, the Ranger cadre specifically told me that had I not done this, they were prepared to give me and the four squad leaders a failing grade. Instead, we all passed this patrol and received our Ranger Tabs at graduation.

Following Ranger training and certification, I was assigned to Schofield Barracks, Hawaii. There I joined the 4th Battalion, 21st Infantry, 11th Light Infantry Brigade for infantry unit training in a jungle environment. Our company commander was Captain David (Dave) O. Treadwell (U.S. Military Academy Class of 1962), and he ranks high among the great leaders I have known. He was a seasoned combat veteran, having had a prior tour in Vietnam, and he understood that many of the gains we made or lands we seized would be abandoned at some point in the not-too-distant future. Dave understood that a major component of his responsibilities was to mentor his lieutenants through counseling and setting an example. He was a firm believer that leadership was the art of getting people to do what must be done despite the circumstances, personal risks, and possible consequences. He clearly cared for the soldiers he led, and under his leadership, I learned the value of truly being responsible for and caring for the men of my command. I was initially too mission focused and slow to fully comprehend how vital this is for a leader, a fault in my foundation which I have earnestly corrected. For his officers, he constantly reminded us that if we focused on taking care of the soldiers, they would follow us into hell and take care of us as well. The first element of caring for soldiers is to make sure they are fully trained, prepared, and ready for anything they may encounter. In Hawaii we conducted rigorous jungle training with a challenging terrain that had steep hills and narrow valleys. Dave set high training standards and drove us hard, and his preparations served us well in ground combat in Vietnam, where he would not foster shortcuts and undue risk. I was originally assigned as an extra lieutenant in the company, as there was a projected vacancy prior to deployment due to performance and disciplinary issues, so I was assigned to the second platoon with another second lieutenant and we would alternate leading the platoon during exercises.

Shortly before deployment, I was assigned to replace the First Platoon leader, while my West Point classmate, Joe Pena, led the Third Platoon. Just a couple of weeks before we deployed, I was blessed to have Sergeant Nick Bacon join my platoon as a squad leader. He had a prior tour in Vietnam with the 1st Infantry Division, he was the same age as I was, and I could easily draw upon his experiences and common sense. We worked closely together, and I would often join his squad for night ambushes and move to contact along with his squad. For the first few months, we operated in the mountains and valleys south of Chu Lai and west of Highway One.

Much to the consternation of my company commander, our battalion commander would observe our operations and the surrounding area from a helicopter flying at 5,000 feet (the normal altitude there to avoid ground fire). We would get messages such as "I see footprints in the sand—go check them out." The only problem is that the only footprints possibly visible from 5,000 feet would be those of elephants, not the Viet Cong or North Vietnamese. Likewise, what looks like a short distance from 5,000 feet is actually a mile or two, often through hostile territory where we would be exposed to punji sticks (sharp bamboo stakes with toxic tips), booby traps, direct fire from the enemy, and multiple other hazards, including the occasional angry water buffalo.

This was not unique to our battalion, and later many of my compatriots and I would refer to this as the "5,000-foot view of things." I have occasionally noticed a similarity in the business world: senior leaders forget that the higher you are in the leadership chain, the less you actually see unless you go down to the action.

After several months, we moved farther north and supported the 196th Infantry Brigade north of Chu Lai. There, we conducted search-and-destroy missions on the coastal plain and in the foothills to the west, where we would look for armed insurgents (Viet Cong) as well as supply caches hidden in the jungle or near villages. If we encountered enemy forces, we would attack, and if we located supplies, we would destroy them and increase the surveillance in that area and set out ambushes (usually after dark) along likely approaches. During this period, my platoon generally had only about twenty-five to thirty soldiers in the field out of the forty authorized. We would be inserted to an area on UH-1 helicopters that would easily hold about six to eight of us with our equipment, with a machine gunner on either side in case we needed covering fire during insertion, though usually we did not. We would walk to the objective and then conduct sweeps in that area of around six to ten kilometers per day. Most of our engagements up to this point were of a limited nature against the Viet Cong.

However, on August 25, 1968, our company was attached to the 1st Squadron, 1st Cavalry (an armored cavalry unit with armored personnel carriers with 50-caliber machine guns and light tanks in support) for combat operations west of Tam Ky. We moved to contact, watching

enemy bullets striking the ground to our front and with tanks and machine guns firing over our heads to support us from along the side of
the armored personnel carriers. We approached the enemy bunker line
until we came within rocket-propelled grenade range, at which time the
tanks and armored vehicles stopped and continued the support firing at
the area of the bunker line. Due to my subsequent wounds, blood loss,
and loss of consciousness, I have only flashes of memories of the events
beyond this point and cannot recall most of the events going forward.
What I have been told is that I led the assault with the First Platoon and
I was near the front of the platoon, while Joe Pena and his platoon were
to my right flank and echeloned slightly to the rear, with the Second Platoon similarly echeloned to the left rear. In retrospect, I believe that what
Captain Treadwell would have wanted and what I should have done
was to hold up or draw back slightly and call for fire support (mortars,
artillery, or bombs) to destroy the enemy rather than to try to do it with
my platoon. This is reinforced by the knowledge that we did not keep
the ground that we had taken and our mission was really to kill as many
of the enemy as possible, not seize the land. Unfortunately, in war, there
are not "do overs."

Apparently, I led the attack with about five other soldiers (a fire team).
We penetrated the enemy bunker line and were in the vicinity of their
command post when I was critically wounded. Joe was similarly posi-
tioned with his platoon and was killed attempting to breach the bunker
line on the right flank by eliminating a machine gun position shortly
thereafter. Nick Bacon took over the lead of my platoon and the lead
of the Third Platoon, rallied both units, and consolidated the attack.
Because of the size of the enemy force and their dug-in position, the company had been ordered to break contact and withdraw so that the jets
could come in with napalm (jelled gasoline) bombs. Nick was ordered to
pull back but refused, stating that he would not leave without his lieutenant and men, even though he was convinced that we most likely had
already been killed. Among my memory flashes are partial consciousness
in an armored personnel carrier in which I was sprawled on top of other
wounded or dead soldiers, and the driver was killed and pulled on top
of me. I also think I either dreamed or was semi-conscious when we
arrived at the helicopter pick-up point, where I think I was apologizing
for fixing the assault by penetrating the bunker line. I also remember

thinking I was freezing when they cut my clothes off in the helicopter. I also remember that sometime after I arrived at the 2d Surgical Hospital in Chu Lai, a bright light was shone in my face and I heard a voice saying "there is not much we can do for this poor boy." This was like a shot of adrenaline, and my eyes opened wide. When asked by someone, I said that I could move my arms and legs, and I squeezed this person's hands with all my might. From there I was whisked to the operating room and recall little else until I somehow found myself in the 85th Evacuation Hospital in Qui Nhon instead of the 2d Surgical Hospital in Chu Lai where I was first evaluated and treated. Many years later, Lieutenant Colonel (Retired) Treadwell told me that they all thought that I was dead when they evacuated me and he essentially had to force the medical evacuation helicopter pilot to take me rather than put me on a later cargo helicopter. He also told me that when they reached the hospital, I had been placed outside with the dead until a medic realized I was alive. I was also told that after the initial recovery and surgery, I was reported back to them as being up, walking with assistance, and visiting with the wounded. The only part of this that I remember is that I did somehow talk to another of my classmates, Hank Berthelot, who had been severely wounded in a different battle nearby and was also in the intensive care unit at the same time.

I do know that Nick Bacon's act of valor saved my life and the lives of others with me. The citation for the Medal of Honor follows:

For conspicuous gallantry and intrepidity in action at the risk of his life above and beyond the call of duty. S/Sgt. Bacon distinguished himself while serving as a squad leader with the 1st Platoon, Company B, during an operation west of Tam Ky. When Company B came under fire from an enemy bunker line to the front, S/Sgt. Bacon quickly organized his men and led them forward in an assault. He advanced on a hostile bunker and destroyed it with grenades. As he did so, several fellow soldiers including the 1st Platoon leader, were struck by machine gun fire and fell wounded in an exposed position forward of the rest of the platoon. S/Sgt. Bacon immediately assumed command of the platoon and assaulted the hostile gun position, finally killing the enemy gun crew in a single-handed effort. When the 3d Platoon moved to S/Sgt. Bacon's location, its leader was also wounded. Without hesitation S/Sgt. Bacon took charge of the additional platoon and continued the fight.

In the ensuing action he personally killed 4 more enemy soldiers and silenced an antitank weapon. Under his leadership and example, the members of both platoons accepted his authority without question. Continuing to ignore the intense hostile fire, he climbed up on the exposed deck of a tank and directed fire into the enemy position while several wounded men were evacuated. As a result of S/Sgt. Bacon's extraordinary efforts, his company was able to move forward, eliminate the enemy positions, and rescue the men trapped to the front. S/Sgt. Bacon's bravery at the risk of his life was in the highest traditions of the military service and reflects great credit upon himself, his unit, and the U.S. Army.

It was Nick Bacon's personal loyalty to me that drove him to go back into the enemy lines to pull me and those that were with me out, even though they had been ordered to withdraw and they were planning to drop napalm bombs on the area. Nick just said, "Sir, I'm not going without my lieutenant," and turned around and went forward. That's about as strong a personal loyalty as you can get.

Nick showed me how to get the best out of everyone and taught me the value of personal loyalty. Everything that I have accomplished since that day I owe to his actions and the sacrifices of others. Today, fifty years later, hardly a day goes by that I do not think of him and his valor. Every year I also honor Joe Pena by a contribution in his name to Disabled Sports, founded by our West Point classmate Doug Pringle, who lost a leg in Vietnam.

I was discharged from Walter Reed Army Medical Center the following year, when I would normally have been assigned to an Infantry Division for duty as a company executive officer and then company commander. However, due to some physical limitations, I was instead assigned to the Advanced Infantry Training Brigade (AIT) at Fort McClellan, Alabama. I initially served on the training committee and taught the elements of jungle warfare to new soldiers and junior leaders, after which I commanded a training company. This became a continuation of the lessons to be learned from observing poor leadership. The training battalion commander was obsessed with statistics regarding training standards and was believed to prefer great fabricated statistics to poorer, but realistic, statistics. This resulted in both noncommissioned officers and officers deliberately overlooking shortfalls. Appearances were more important than performance. Concern for the well-being of trainees was not paramount, and recycling poor performers to a following class was extremely difficult, if not impossible.

While I was a patient at Walter Reed Army Medical Center, one of my treating physicians had informed me of a new program in the Army to select young officers to attend medical school as their military assignment. My original academic interest at West Point was to seek graduate training in chemical engineering, so I had taken organic and physical chemistry as my two elective courses. Thus, I had already completed the majority of premedical requirements. I had set this information aside in my mind, planning to either continue as an infantry officer or see if I could figure out a way to attend flight school despite my lack of perfect vision. However, what I saw in terms of leadership in the AIT Brigade caused me to reconsider this, and I completed my pre-medical requirements through evening classes at Jacksonville State University. I was subsequently granted admission to Emory University School of Medicine, and I was accepted by the Army for fully funded attendance as an Army officer. (Of course, this added five more years of obligated service to my initial four years for attendance at West Point.) The following year, I set my leadership aspirations aside and headed off to medical school.

As a medical student, I was consumed by my studies and was focused on obtaining a medical degree rather than developing as a leader. However, I continued to observe leadership in action, and there were two particular leaders among the faculty that stood out. The first was my primary mentor, Dr. Louis J. (Skip) Elsas, the chair of Medical Genetics. He was an inspiring lecturer and brought his subject to life with examples of real people and the consequences of genetic diseases on themselves and their children. He was one of the pioneers in biochemical genetics, and the Army allowed me to remain at Emory during the summers between my last two years to work with him. He reinforced the personal aspect of concern for those you lead and those you serve. He was a technical expert in his field and working with him I was able to have two papers published, present them at a regional conference, and receive an award from the Southern Society for Pediatric Research. From him I learned the importance of functional area expertise, meticulous attention to detail, and personal commitment to a higher cause. I did not work as closely with the other great leader, Dr. H. Kenneth (Ken) Walker, but I was profoundly impressed by his personal, sincere interest in, and sage advice to, each individual medical student rotating through his service. He took each of us to a nice restaurant in Atlanta, and ascertained from each of us both what we thought were the good points of the program and what we thought might improve it. He also queried our ambitions and provided advice concerning future training and experiences. He offered suggestions and expressed a willingness to help us reach our goals. From him I developed a better understanding of the value stemming from a personal commitment between a leader and each individual on the team.

After graduation, I was promoted to major (based on time in grade as a captain) and became an intern/first-year resident in pediatrics at Letterman Army Medical Center (LAMC) on the Presidio of San Francisco. In this capacity, I was focused on the clinical training and had little opportunity or exposure for development as a leader. What I did discover was something that should have been obvious: pediatrics was not an essential specialty for the military. As those of us in pediatrics scrambled for limited resources, there was abundant support for internal medicine and the surgical specialties. Near the end of the first year, the rotation for pediatric residents to Thailand for the study of infectious diseases at the Army Tropical Medicine Research Institute was canceled for lack of funding. Despite my love for pediatric medicine, given that I already had a substantial service obligation to the Army for my time at West Point and in medical school, I decided to abandon this study and seek training in a field of greater value to the Army. In the interim, I was given the opportunity to train as a flight surgeon and serve as the Command Surgeon for the Commanding General (CG) of the 193d Infantry Brigade and Canal Zone in Panama (a position which called for a lieutenant colonel—preferably an experienced one; I was neither). This turned out to be a fortuitous choice that served as the commencement of my career as a leader in the Army Medical Department (AMEDD).

My medical experience base at that time consisted of five months as a patient, four years at a civilian medical school, and one year as a pediatric intern with no actual military responsibilities, as I was caring for infants and children. I had completed the Infantry Officer Basic Course (for lieutenants), but not the AMEDD Officer Basic Course, and neither the Advanced Infantry nor Medical Officer Courses (for captains). Other than my experiences as a combat casualty, I had no idea how the

AMEDD fit in military organizations and supported ground forces. The Flight Surgeon Course did give me a great introduction to the primary military medical and physical evaluation regulations; the importance of altitude physiology, from high pressures under water to high-altitude, low-pressure flight; and the role of the helicopter in support of Army ground operations. To my delight, I also learned the fundamentals of flight and rotary wing aircraft and was given sufficient training to lift off, move from point A to point B, and land a helicopter (as long as there was an actual pilot accompanying me in case anything went wrong with the aircraft).

Shortly after my arrival in the Canal Zone, I discovered that I was woefully unprepared for my assigned duties, particularly given my rank. This was at a critical juncture in time, as negotiations to return the Canal Zone to Panama were initiated and there was concern that a conflict could develop if these negotiations failed. Potential reactions range from sabotage of the locks to unconventional warfare and destruction of the earthen dams. My responsibilities included the clinical oversight of four troop medical clinics staffed by physician assistants (two at each end of the canal, with one on each side of, and some distance from, the canal); oversight of the aviation medicine program supporting the aviation battalion with one flight surgeon (Dr. Cliff Patterson, a classmate at the Aviation Medicine Basic Course); staff oversight of a separate medical company designed to resuscitate, stabilize, and evacuate soldiers in support of a single brigade in combat; formalize the medical logistics program; and write the medical annex for combat operations to defend the canal. Clinical and staff oversight in this setting means that, while none of the leaders in these settings reported to me, I would be held accountable for their decisions and actions. With no coercive capability in this setting, I had to become a master at leadership through influence, which was also to serve me well as I became more senior in organizations and more distant from where actions were occurring. The only metaphor that I can conjure up for the extensive requirements that I faced would be that I could either stand at the bottom of the deep end of a pool and watch the bubbles rise while I drowned or work my way to the surface and learn to swim in a hurry.

I came up with a short-term solution to meet my initial needs. At the end of every week, I would write down the tasks that I felt needed to be accomplished the following week and ranked them in priority as I saw it. I then took this list to Colonel Jim Franklin, the deputy brigade commander; reviewed it with him; and asked him to verify the tasks, add or delete items, and revise the order of my priorities to meet the needs of the command. He was a patient and outstanding mentor who allowed me to articulate my rationale for the tasks to be accomplished and my proposed sequence. He would reinforce my thoughts when on target, add to the list, and explain to me where I appeared to be missing the point. Doing this served me extraordinarily well, and as I learned over time, he had less to add and our priorities were closer in order. Since then I have recommended this process to many others.

It rapidly became obvious to me that a baseline of knowledge was essential, but I could not possibly develop true expertise in any single area in the prescribed time. Therefore I sought sufficient familiarity with the subject matter that I could ensure a logical and progressive level of expertise to avoid being fooled by false self-proclaimed expertise of others with differing agendas. This proved to be a rational course. Fortunately, the AMEDD Center and School had multiple correspondence courses that covered this information that I needed but they were to be taken in a set order which did not account for my urgent need. Exams and results were to be mailed back and forth between Panama and San Antonio through the U.S. Postal Service. Given the urgency of the situation, with the help of a few senior leaders I was able to obtain the course material in a selective rather than prescribed order, and I got through it as rapidly as possible without bothering with grades. As I worked through the course material I became progressively more aware of what needed to be accomplished for success daily as well as for contingency planning, and I targeted my studies accordingly.

Early in this assignment, I also became aware of a disconnect between the line command, responsible for operational medical readiness, and the Army Medical Department Activity (MEDDAC), responsible for the delivery of day-to-day health services to soldiers and their families. I quickly realized I was caught in the middle. This was compounded by the fact that Gorgas Hospital was an institution of the Canal Zone Government, but key positions were actually held by active duty Army Medical Corps officers who provided specialty services and hospital support to Canal Zone civilians as well as the military. In addition, there was a smaller hospital at Coco Solo on the Atlantic side. For a variety of reasons, both hospitals held untenable positions for use in armed conflict, so this became a major planning factor. The Commanding General, Major General William R. Richardson (who later became the Commanding General of the Army Training and Doctrine Command), sent me back to the United States to meet with line and AMEDD leaders to determine how the relationship between the combat forces and the AMEDD was supposed to work in terms of resource sharing, logistics, and contingency operations. Bringing this information back to Major General (MG) Richardson did not endear me to certain elements of the AMEDD leadership with a different agenda, but it did result in curtailing the MEDDAC commander's tour and beginning the development of a more productive relationship and team effort with his successor. The field medical company was placed under my operational control, which changed the relationship from advising to directing, and we developed a viable logistics structure, capable of field distribution, while sharing selected assets with the MEDDAC, generating significant cost savings for both. Ultimately, I developed sufficient expertise to develop, write, and obtain command approval for the medical annex to the operations plan for the defense of the Canal Zone. This annex included identifying the types of medical units required, proposed locations, and support requirements for their operations, as well as timelines for field medical units to be inserted to react to an imminent threat to the Canal Zone.

General Richardson was one of my great mentors. He understood my background, encouraged and supported my personal training program, was open to my ideas, and gave me the senior leadership support that I needed. He was one of the most effective teachers/trainers that I have had the opportunity to observe as he worked with soldiers, and I recognized that technical and tactical proficiency and the ability to evaluate and communicate individual and collective skill are critical capabilities for leaders. I valued his trust in me and strived even harder not to let him down. From him I learned the value of inspirational leadership.

During my time in Panama, I visited regularly with the Army physicians on the staff to see the different specialties in action outside of an academic setting. I particularly enjoyed my time with the general surgeons, and they allowed me to observe or assist in several cases. Ultimately, I decided to apply for surgical training in the Army and was selected to return to

Letterman Army Medical Center as a resident in general surgery. However, due to the critical nature of my duties, my departure from the Canal Zone was delayed until a suitable replacement was on site and had been thoroughly briefed on the operational planning process, the rationale for the written medical annex, and every contingency site visited. Because of this, I started and graduated from my surgical residency two months late, an accommodation that Army Medicine, as opposed to a civilian program, could make without too much difficulty. However, the expression "no good deed goes unpunished" comes to mind, as the delay caused me to be on a different timetable than my contemporaries. The program was short a resident for two months, it had problems in coordinating rotations, there was an extra "chief resident" for two months at the end, and I graduated late, resulting in a shortage at my first assignment.

A general surgery residency was four years of structured training following the internship, during which the resident physician would assume increasing responsibilities for patients with more complex surgical conditions and progressive leadership of the surgical team. At Letterman Army Medical Center (LAMC), the first three years of this training included rotations through other surgical specialties such as urology and orthopedic surgery, surgical intensive care, complicated burns (at the Institute for Surgical Research at Fort Sam Houston, Texas), intense hands-on surgical experience (at Silas B. Hays Army Community Hospital—SBHAH—on Fort Ord, near Monterey, California), and trauma surgery at the San Francisco General Hospital. My final year was as chief resident, leading a team of interns and junior and senior residents under the direct supervision of an attending academic, board-certified surgeon.

During my first of two four-month surgical rotations at Fort Ord, I met Captain Ann Erickson, who arrived at the start of January 1979 from the Pediatric Nurse Practitioner program at Fitzsimons Army Medical Center in Aurora, Colorado, and was assigned to the inpatient pediatric service at SBHAH. We were married in the LAMC hospital chapel a year and a half later, once she completed her tour on active duty at Fort Ord.

At Letterman, there was a large, permanent support staff, and as I increased in responsibility each year, I had to draw on resources from other departments, which helped me learn about the role of unofficial influencers in an organization. Regrettably, this beautiful facility no longer exists, as the Presidio of San Francisco was closed in the 1990s. On the top five floors at the end of the hospital toward the bay, each ward had a sunroom projecting off each floor. From there, from the east solariums, the Palace of Fine Arts and waterfront could be seen to the right along with the bay and Alcatraz. From the west you could see the Presidio, Fort Mason, the Golden Gate Bridge, and Fort Baker across the bay. These solariums were primarily for the inpatients during the day, but in the early morning, after a night on call, the medical and surgical residents and staff would frequently gather in one of the tenth-floor solariums and watch the sunrise to the east and then watch to the west as the sun illuminated the Golden Gate Bridge. The fog rolled in under the bridge as the foghorns began to sound.

Colonel (later Brigadier General) John E. Hutton was the Chief of General and Peripheral Vascular Surgery at Letterman Army Medical Center during my training. He was a true gentleman scholar with a variety of interests. Of particular note was his eye for photography, leading to a number of his photographs being used on the cover of *Yachting Magazine*. He was an ideal role model—composed, gracious, and concerned for the well-being of our patients and his staff and residents. He was extraordinarily calm under pressure. One of the greatest potential catastrophes in vascular surgery is when an abdominal aortic aneurysm ruptures after the abdominal cavity has been opened. Within seconds, the entire cavity fills with blood and the patient can bleed to death in seconds. This occurred on more than one occasion, given the patient population we served, but when it happened, Dr. Hutton would react immediately, reach in with his hand and compress the aorta above the rupture, stopping the bleeding, then calmly direct the anesthesia staff to push fluids and blood as rapidly as possible, and finally pause and announce to the operating team "we're in the soup now, folks!" He would then, in a clear and measured voice, give concise instructions to each member of the team. He never showed signs of panic, and his calm demeanor allowed each member to proceed in an orderly manner. You could feel your own pulse dropping back to normal so you could concentrate on fixing the problem. As a person, surgeon, and leader, he was respected and admired by all.

I contrast this with another senior member of the surgery faculty who, whenever even the slightest thing went wrong in the operating room, would start screaming, make insulting and intimidating comments to physicians and nurses involved in the procedure, throw instruments, and even reach across the table and strike members of the operating crew. This heightened the anxiety in cases of a similar magnitude to the ones handled so calmly by Dr. Hutton to the extent that staff members would start to tremble and try to work with unsteady hands, making the situation even worse.

The wrong behavior by a leader can and frequently will make a situation worse. It is equivalent to pouring gasoline on a fire. I carried this lesson throughout the remainder of my surgical career as well as my career as a leader.

As I progressed in responsibility at LAMC, I became aware of a factor that I had either not encountered or had been unaware of in my prior roles as a combat arms officer or a medical student. This is the impact that those I refer to as "the unofficial influencers" can have on an organization. They can be at found at every level in an organization, and they can, and often do, disrupt resource allocation and operational efficiency inside or outside of their functional area or what should be their area of interest. Over time, they become the "go-to person," which provides an illusion of power and ego gratification. They reluctantly grant as a "favor" that which should be offered without question, or they divert resources which are outside of their purview by trading favors for such, even if these resources are designated for another purpose, thereby disrupting a different functional area. Until I realized that these were assumed roles, not assigned roles, and had a negative impact, I became quite effective at finding these people and leveraging their support.

There are some highly successful organizations with a flat organizational structure, but they are the minority and generally are composed of highly talented, self-started individuals firmly vested in the organization. For most organizations, however, there is a defined hierarchy for very good reasons, including the establishment and maintenance of clear unit and sub-unit missions and the efficient utilization of resources which can be more rapidly and efficiently distributed according to varying mission requirements. In hierarchical organizations, missions and responsibilities can be adjusted quickly when driven by demand. In this setting, responsibilities are clearly defined and leaders are held accountable throughout the organization, through the executives to the governing body.

Later in my career I became aware that "unofficial influencers" were not unique to LAMC but exist in many organizations of varying types, military and civilian, and they can be found at multiple levels. I have even noted senior leaders engaged in this behavior for their own ends, at the expense of others and the overall corporate welfare. The blame for resulting failures falls upon other accountable leaders, and in doing so, undermines them. While some of this behavior may not cause any significant harm, all of these activities impact organizational efficiency and some cause tremendous damage in both employee morale and corporate welfare. I have concluded that wherever and whenever they are identified, both the influencer and the influenced need to be confronted by senior leadership and formally cautioned that this will not be tolerated. Whether it appears to be innocent or completely self-serving is irrelevant. It will ultimately adversely impact organizational efficiency.

During my surgical residency I was selected to attend the Army Command and General Staff College. However, these studies were deferred, as it was more important for me to gain experience in a surgical practice and complete certification by the American Board of Surgery. Therefore, following my service-delayed graduation from the surgical residency, I was assigned to Reynolds Army Community Hospital at Fort Sill, Oklahoma (near Lawton). As the surgeon that I was to replace had departed in early summer, the hospital had been short a general surgeon for over three months and had not been given an explanation for my delay. Fortunately, I had a good reputation and there were others present who confirmed that the delay was not due to academic issues, but was for the benefit of the Army. I arrived on a Sunday in mid-September and reported to the hospital the following morning, where I was informed that, as I was a lieutenant colonel, I was now the chief of general surgery despite coming straight out of training. I was also provided three already scheduled cases for surgery the following morning and would have to do the preoperative history, physical exam, and counseling that evening. Fortunately, my wife had remained in San Francisco to finish her Master of Science in Nursing (MSN) at the University of California in San Francisco, so I was temporarily in the bachelor officers' quarters and she and I did not have to set up a household immediately.

The first year at Fort Sill was an exciting time for us. Our surgical group worked well together and took on many challenging cases, taking on the full scope of general surgery, including some vascular and non-cardiac thoracic surgery. My primary partner there was Dr. R. Lawrence (Larry) Reed, and he led and modernized the Surgical Intensive Care Unit (SICU) with my assistance. We were constantly busy and highly regarded by our colleagues. The command structure was very supportive and the nursing service performed at a high level. Ann completed her MSN program and joined the faculty of Cameron University in Lawton. The chief nurse, whom we both thought highly of and was supportive to the staff and easy to work with, encouraged Ann to leave Cameron and return to active duty to take the head nurse position in pediatrics, which she did. Unfortunately, we were not aware that this chief nurse was departing and there would shortly be a new chief nurse with an entirely different agenda, leading Ann to resign her commission. This worked out well, however, as a close friend of mine from my tour in the Canal Zone, Colonel Carmello Fabrigar, was already stationed there when we arrived. His wife, Pauline, served as Ann's first mentor in the transition to her future role as an Army leader's spouse as I progressed in my career. We were to serve close to them in our subsequent tours in Europe.

That summer, the commander and chief nurse both transferred and the entire command climate changed for the worse. I relate this here because it is the single best example of the impact of poor leadership on an organization that I have observed. The new commander, whom I had admired for years and who had served very effectively as the clinical deputy, proved less effective in command because he would listen only to his deputies, who had different agendas and were providing him with poor advice. The new clinical deputy had a conflict of interest due to a relationship with a nearby community hospital that made it difficult to enforce standards for clinicians, the administrative deputy did not appear particularly supportive of the clinical staff, and the chief nurse appeared to have priorities other than topnotch clinical care. Rules were instituted that were nonsensical and contrary to good practice. For example, to give a crisper, more uniform exterior appearance, all window shades had to be set at the same height at all times. For most patients, this is not a problem, but for pediatric patients taking naps and eye surgery patients recovering from surgery, it was inappropriate. As a surgeon, I was able to bypass this order by writing a clinical order for a darkened room for my patients needing to rest, but this did not sit well with the hospital leadership.

Dr. Reed and I adapted our surgical scheduling practice so that we would first look at the nursing shift schedule so that we would know when the most competent nurses would be working on the critical nights following our big cases. The chief nurse decided it would be more "efficient" to consolidate the surgical intensive care unit, which was adjacent to the operating suites, with the coronary care unit four stories higher and at the other end of the building, away from the operating rooms, so that postoperative patients could be monitored with black-and-white video cameras rather than bedside nurses.

In preparation, she had moved some of the critical care nurses from the ICU to various clinics, creating an artificial staffing crisis, and submitted a decision paper to the commander to effect this change on the day I left town for two weeks of temporary duty. Fortunately, Dr. Reed and I had already gotten wind of her intentions and I was prepared to act if she attempted to do this. When I was notified that this proposal was submitted for decision before my return, I called the surgical consultant at the Office of the Army Surgeon General and let him know what was happening and what I was planning to do, so he would be prepared for any reaction. I then called the commander with the names, specialties, and locations of the hidden nurses. The commander did immediately stop the consolidation but was annoyed with me even though I had previously attempted to let him know what was being planned.

The chief nurse could not touch me so she decided to punish my wife for my behavior. The senior nursing staff, obviously with the chief nurse's support, already had an established pattern of punishing my wife for my behavior (such as ordering a darkened room from 1:00 to 3:00 p.m. so my pediatric patients could nap) by pulling her staff to other areas, deliberately leaving her short-handed taking care of small children. After defeating the ICU consolidation project, this got so bad that Ann had to let parents know that their children likely would not be fed unless they came to the hospital over the lunch hour to feed them, which was not well accepted in the community. The final straw for Ann came when the head nurse of the emergency room, located fifty feet from my office, called Ann, who was five floors away, to let her know that she had not received the new surgical call schedule and demanded that she provide her the schedule, threatening to just put my name on the board until she got one. Unfortunately for her, my wife responded first by assuring her that she would have one soon and then walked into the command suite, letting the Deputy Commander for Clinical Services and the Commander know exactly what happened, why it happened, and the pattern of harassment she had been subjected to by the nursing leadership. Shortly thereafter, the senior noncommissioned officer from the emergency room walked the fifty feet down the hall to get a copy form the surgical secretary. Ann discussed this with me at home, and she decided to submit her immediate resignation, citing maternity, which they had to honor in accordance with the Army regulations at that time.

This assignment reinforced the lesson that I had learned at Fort McClellan: ineffective or toxic leadership at the top can have a devastating effect on an entire organization. During this assignment I learned that success at one level does not automatically lead to success at the next level. I also learned the importance of listening to everyone and not just to immediate subordinates (or direct reports). The priority of a few of the leaders appeared to be more focused on appearances than on quality healthcare services, and the less care that is delivered the better superficial appearances may be. Not all of one's advisors have the same priorities, and some may have other (likely hidden) agendas that may ultimately work against a responsible leader. The result is dysfunction and poor morale, but the leader is the one who should be held accountable.

Concomitantly, I had been in personal discussions with the Army Surgeon General (TSG), Lieutenant General (LTG) Bernhard Mittemeyer, who had approached me concerning an initiative that was very important to him. Historically, medical battalions in Army maneuver divisions had been commanded by Medical Corps officers (physicians), but for the previous decade, Medical Service Corps officers (administrators and aviators) had commanded these organizations in peacetime with a plan to replace them with Medical Corps officers upon deploying for actual patient care. A medical battalion consisted of a headquarters and service company with a "clearing station," which is a treatment facility for basic resuscitation and stabilization before further evacuation, and an ambulance platoon to evacuate casualties from the forward clearing stations. There were also three forward medical companies with a similar mission, except their ambulances would evacuate from the forward maneuver battalion aid stations to the main clearing station for further evacuation. In peacetime, only simulated casualties are treated, but in combat operations, these stations care for actual wounded soldiers. LTG Mittemeyer was concerned that training was too often focused on the operational issues, with minimal focus on the clinical care required. He had selected me, based upon my background and experience (particularly in the Canal Zone), to be the first Medical Corps officer to take on such a command, with the intent to have up to one-fourth of the medical battalion commanders be from the Medical Corps. Our discussions were well underway when Ann resigned. This made it easier for me to depart Fort Sill early, and after negotiations with the Army Chief of Staff and other senior general officers, LTG Mittemeyer nominated me to become the Division Surgeon for the Commanding General (CG) of the 8th Infantry Division, headquartered in Bad Kreuznach, Germany, for a year with a programmed follow-on assignment as the Commander of the 3d Medical Battalion in Giebelstadt, Germany. In preparation for this assignment, I was given the opportunity to learn about the Army method for vehicle and equipment evaluation and maintenance through a course for projected commanders of mechanized organizations. I first met Major Gary Kindred at this course, and we became friends as he helped me to understand many of the intricacies of vehicle maintenance.

In May 1983, Ann and I departed for Germany, visiting relatives along the way as I had done so often with my parents as a child of a military family. Other than for short courses and eleven months at the Army War College in Carlisle Barracks, Pennsylvania, we remained in Germany until 1992, and our two daughters and our son were born there.

We arrived in Frankfurt after an overnight flight on a completely full Pan Am airplane (generally referred to by military families as the cattle car, as it was always packed to capacity) when Ann was seven months along in her pregnancy and not comfortable. On arrival, I greeted her with a birthday card and a lame comment about a trip to Europe for her birthday, by which she was not amused. We were greeted at the airport by members of my new staff and transported to Bad Kreuznach. We were to spend several weeks that summer—the hottest in recent history—in a fourth-floor walk-up apartment with our pet Weimaraner, who needed to be walked at least three times per day. Fortunately, within about a month, we moved into a government-leased duplex townhouse in the small village of Pfaffen-Schwabenheim not far out of Bad Kreuznach.

This was an exciting time for us. Bad Kreuznach is a beautiful city, famous for its bridge houses over the Nahe River as it flows through the town. Along the river are the Salinentals, stacks of reeds through which water flows, releasing mineral salts into the air and making it a relaxing place to stroll. The surrounding countryside is covered with grape vines. On Fridays the Division Headquarters would have a fun run where we would be bused to the hill sides and run through the vineyards, along the Nahe River, through the Salinentals, and up the hill by the military hospital, and then end at the officer's club. My older brother, Linwood III, and his wife, Elfi, lived in Wurzburg, where he was a Department of Defense Dependents School (DoDDS) teacher, and my younger brother, Jack, was an officer on the U.S. Army Europe (USAREUR) staff in Heidelberg, where he lived with his wife, Cathy, and son, John. Our daughter Carolyn was born in August at the Wiesbaden Hospital where I was on the adjunct staff as a general surgeon, and all three families were able to get together frequently.

Our first few weeks included the Army's Gateway to Germany language class for both of us, as well as studying German/European traffic laws and signs to obtain USAREUR driver's licenses. I also performed my required flight physical and aviation orientation in order to return to flying status as a flight surgeon. After that, I spent the next month traveling around the area with my predecessor, then LTC Dan Perugini. The 8th Infantry Division (8ID) was dispersed over central Germany, with units in Baumholder to the west, Wiesbaden to the north, Manheim to the southeast, and Wildflecken to the east. In an unusual set of circumstances, not only was our daughter Carolyn born that summer, but the Commanding General's wife had a new baby, as did another senior staff officer's wife. The three mothers got together frequently with the children that year.

During this tour I had four particular mentors who were critical to my later successes. First was LTC Jim Wortham, an MSC officer commanding the 8th Medical Battalion. He gave me the best orientation to medical battalion command and identified the critical duties and relationships. It was essentially a personal tutorial on every aspect from battalion operations to maintenance, logistics, and military personnel management while his wife Penny tutored Ann on her transition from Army Nurse Corps officer to spouse of a forward-stationed battalion commander. They were the most gracious couple we have had the pleasure to serve with and be mentored by. This was particularly noteworthy because Jim did so with some peril, as there was considerable angst within the MSC leadership regarding LTG Mittemeyer's initiative to restore Medical Corps leadership in the maneuver divisions. He also cautioned me that his contemporary currently commanding the 3d Medical Battalion, which I was to command, had urged the 3d Infantry Division Commanding General to fight my assignment all the way to the Chief of Staff of the Army, which he did without success.

At the onset of the Cold War, there was a robust American military presence in West Germany. However, with the war in Vietnam and the high expenses associated with this forward presence, American forces were gradually reduced and replaced with an annual "Return of Forces to Germany (REFORGER)" exercise. This would generally involve the deployment of a full division (15,000–20,000 soldiers) and a force-on-force exercise lasting up to a month. I had previously participated in such an exercise as a general surgeon, where due to location and weather conditions I had actually performed surgery in a combat support hospital set up in the field in northern Germany.

This year the 8th Infantry Division was a participating unit in the force-on-force operation, and I had the opportunity to provide the staff coordination and oversight for the medical support of the division. In my role, I regularly interfaced with LTC Wortham, and he assisted me by providing fantastic on-the-job training for my next role as a medical battalion commander, walking me through the establishment of the clearing stations and the system for establishing a ground ambulance deployment system that carried medical supplies forward to the battalion aid stations and returned with casualties.

Assigned to my staff as the Division Psychiatrist was CPT Herbert (Bert) Price, who partnered with the Division Social Worker, CPT Gene Wilkinson, to conduct the first "Psych Ex," in which they led a team to work with casualties and Post Traumatic Stress Disorder patients generated by a mass casualty situation. This was before the Army leadership was fully engaged with these issues, and this work was on the cutting edge of the tenets of behavior health for casualties: proximity (treat forward), immediacy (rest, food, and early counseling), and expectancy (plan to return to duty quickly). Dr. Price later served with me in Augsburg as Chief of Behavioral Health. After leaving the Army, he had settled in

Jonesboro, Arkansas, and he was the first physician that I recruited to be a regional medical director when I became the Chief Medical Officer of Arkansas Blue Cross and Blue Shield, based on his combination of expertise in both behavioral health and general medicine.

I was also fortunate to later have LTC Wilkinson on my staff at the 98th General Hospital, as he had proven to be one of the best social workers I had encountered in my career.

LTC David Arthur was the Assistant Chief of Staff for Personnel (G1) during my tenure with the 8ID. Normally, the Division Surgeon would report through the G1 and Chief of Staff to the Commanding General, but as I was senior in grade, I reported directly to the Chief of Staff, Colonel (later General and Chief of Staff of the Army) Dennis Reimer. However, Dave was another great mentor who understood military operations at the division level. I always sought Dave's advice when preparing an initiative or response, and he would bring out the questions likely to occur and walk me through potential scenarios. On Dave's wall was a picture of Oblio, a character from a fairy tale in which a round-headed child must navigate the "Land of Point," where everyone had a pointed head but him. After a series of encounters in his search for the "pointless man," he finds him and discovers that he has a point coming out of his body in every direction from the top of his head to his toes. When questioned by Oblio, the pointless man explains, "A point in every direction is the same as no point at all." This is a great lesson for evolving leaders and advisors. I have used that quote at least once in every subsequent leadership position when counseling my staff and leaders reporting to me regarding concise and focused proposals. As with other mentors, I have never forgotten Dave's support to me in the 8ID.

Colonel Reimer was another outstanding leader and mentor during this formative period of my career. He was incredibly patient and would provide guidance in a manner that would be easy to understand and would avoid nonproductive efforts. Being new to this role and lacking the normal requisite military education and training, I made occasional mistakes and inadvertently did not follow proper protocol. In each case, he would patiently explain the error, provide more-detailed guidance, and inspire me to learn from the event and execute to the maximum going forward. Consequently, I never made the same mistake twice.

There were many areas of focus that the Commanding General, MG

(later LTG) Charles W. Dyke, emphasized. First among these was a focus on the families and the sacrifices and contributions that they made
to the military communities across the 8th Infantry Division's area of
responsibility. At the height of the Cold War, a high state of readiness
was an imperative. This focused on training but also required a heavy
focus on material readiness. Much of our equipment and many of our
vehicles were older that the soldiers operating them. MG Dyke made
sure everyone understood that if you cannot get to the battlefield, you
cannot fight. He reminded everyone of the greater cost of delayed maintenance and created an increased emphasis on maintenance and logistics. His Operational Readiness briefings were renowned for their level
of detail on maintenance of vehicles and equipment, and they provided
invaluable lessons for me in my future assignment commanding the 3d
Medical Battalion. He also emphasized the need for constant vigilance
in safety, reminding us all that nothing we do in peacetime warrants
the loss of life or limb. This was particularly noteworthy, as this was at a
time when Soviet forces in the East would accept a 10% casualty rate for
routine training exercises.

MG Dyke also had a strict rule that I have adopted in every leadership
position I have held since then. Specifically, no one must ever preempt
his decision-making capability or authority by deliberately not telling
him something that he should know. He stressed that there is no such
thing as "plausible deniability," as it is really a myth. The best defense is
to make the right decision up front by knowing all the facts so you can
address a critical action or situation prospectively, making an informed
decision rather than having to act in a reactive manner.

The following May we moved to Wurzburg so that I could assume command of the 3d Medical Battalion. At my initial interview with MG
Howard Crowell, the Division Commanding General, he first greeted
me with "welcome to the lion's den" and then explained to me that he
had resisted my assignment because, although I was highly qualified for
this, he was concerned that other Medical Corps officers to follow would
not be so. He had come to understand that in 1969 the Army leadership
had made a decision to fund combat arms officers—particularly those
with experience in Vietnam—to attend medical school and that restoring
a limited number of us to battalion command positions was a byproduct
of this decision and was designed to enhance medical support of combat

forces. He let me know that the decision was made and that he would treat me the same as every other battalion commander in the division, and he did exactly that.

This was followed by a meeting with the Division Support Command (DISCOM) Commander, Colonel Paul J. Vanderploog. At this time, the DISCOM included the Headquarters element and six battalions: the 3d Medical Battalion, the 3d Support and Transportation Battalion, the 703d Maintenance Battalion, and three Forward Support Battalions. It was commanded by a seasoned Colonel (later Major General) Quartermaster Corps officer, who proved to be the best commander and leadership mentor of my career. At our initial interview, he gave me a copy of his command philosophy and provided specific guidance as to his expectations. He encouraged me to set and enforce the highest standards in the battalion and to understand the scope of my authority and act to the full extent thereof. I have given this guidance to others in every leadership position since then.

At every encounter that I had with Colonel Vanderploog, he provided additional guidance in a manner that I best describe as sound bites for leadership, which I would refer to going forward as "VDPisms," and I have passed these on in a similar manner to those I have been privileged to lead. He lived by his philosophy and was consistent in establishment and maintenance of the highest standards of discipline and performance. He was tough, highly knowledgeable in his profession, and firm but fair in his dealings with us. He believed in working hard and playing hard. In the 3ID, we worked hard but we also were able and expected to focus on our families. As leaders, we had a busy social schedule including informal and formal dinners in a variety of settings, including a castle. The most memorable ski trips of my life were in Austria, Switzerland, and France with the group of us, our spouses, and other 3d Infantry Division senior leaders.

In the Army, a battalion commander has far more responsibilities than a junior business executive—and sometimes senior. Not only is such a commander responsible for a specific mission, such as "be prepared for, and on order move to a specified area and execute combat-health-services support to 18,000 soldiers in a forward deployed location," which was the mission of the 3d Medical Battalion, but in garrison a junior commander is responsible for the welfare of the assigned soldiers and their families, maintenance of both wheeled and tracked vehicles, oversight of personnel management, and administration of the Uniform Code of Military Justice. To accomplish this, battalion commanders have a staff which includes an Executive Officer, a Personnel Officer (S1), an Intelligence Officer (S2), an Operations and Training Officer (S3), and a Logistics Officer (S4). Rounding out the staff is the senior enlisted noncommissioned officer, the Battalion Command Sergeant Major who serves as the eyes and ears of the commander, particularly in regard to the morale and discipline of the enlisted soldiers.

My Executive Officer was Major Gary Kindred, who with his wife, Barbara, provided tremendous support for me. I had met Gary at the Preventive Maintenance Course at Fort Knox, Kentucky, and he kept me abreast of the political intrigue prior to my arrival. As Barbara was a native German, now American, she was not only Ann's best friend and shopping consultant, but she helped me with German on several occasions in which I had to deliver a speech both in English and German. She would translate the speech into one that would appear to be written by someone native to the country or completely fluent, and would rehearse me until I had the expressions and pronunciation correct. She would then stick close to me and intercept questions, as I was barely conversant in the language. Ann and Barbara worked closely together to create a great family-oriented social environment for the battalion families. This included social gatherings as well as visits to the battalion in the field, where they could see the soldiers in action and better understand the mission.

During my year in command, the battalion participated in the REFORGER annual exercise opposing a Continental United States (CONUS)-based division. This was a fantastic experience in that we were able to provide actual medical support to the 3d ID and establish clearing stations behind each maneuver brigade and provide minor trauma and initial acute illness care. My headquarters were established in the woods near Adelsried, a small village near Augsburg, in southern Germany, and we were visited frequently by senior observers and received high praise. I must give great credit to my battalion staff and the meticulous planning and execution under Gary Kindred's leadership, to my company commanders for their superb execution, and to Jim Wortham for his past mentoring of me.

During subsequent months under my command through the superb planning and execution efforts of a great staff and outstanding company commanders, we transitioned from establishing triage, resuscitation, and stabilization units in tents and ground support with wheeled ambulances to using five-ton trucks with expandable sides which allowed for the establishment of clearing stations in a cleaner and more standardized setting. We also added fifteen armored, tracked ambulances. These modernization efforts greatly expanded maintenance and training requirements associated with the trucks and tracked vehicles.

Something I did not realize happened during this time was to have an unanticipated personal impact for several years, the consequences of which were to shape my future. Specifically, I had a tick bite on my right shin that did not appear to be significant at the time but was to become quite troublesome later.

I was promoted to colonel during my last three months in command of the battalion and was transferred to the 34th General Hospital in Augsburg, to lead the department of surgery. This was a challenging assignment, as I encountered what I perceived to be one of the worst leadership and command climates in my career during the first year there. From the onset, for arguably the nicest U.S. military location in southern Bavaria, the morale was surprisingly low and the cohesiveness that I had observed in prior assignments was completely lacking. At my first office visit, the commander, instead of communicating his philosophy and expectations, told me that he did not want me there, had tried to have me sent elsewhere, and believed that the AMEDD leadership would never have wasted a good surgeon on assignments with the combat arms. Consequently he intended to have an older lieutenant colonel fill that position. He was clearly annoyed when I pointed out that I was, in fact, a colonel, a board-certified general surgeon, and a fellow of the American College of Surgeons, which affirmed my clinical competency, and it was against Army policy for me to be subordinate to an officer of a lower rank. Furthermore, I pointed out that I had been hand-picked by the Army Surgeon General for both of these assignments and that the Commanding General of the 7th Medical Command (MEDCOM) had specifically told me that I was being sent there to be the Chief of Surgery. His initial response was "we'll see about that," and a few hours later (obviously after he had his fingers burned by actually questioning my assignment with 7th MEDCOM), he informed me that I would be the Chief of Surgery but that one of the general surgeons would work outside of the department and report directly to him so he could independently determine if I knew what I was doing in the operating room. Rather than pushing any further, I simply went ahead and started work.

About a month later, I was called to the intensive care unit to consult on a patient, an older woman traveling with her retired Army husband. She had been admitted with ascites (abdominal fluid) that was allegedly being caused by liver failure. I talked to her and her husband, reviewed her history and laboratory work, and did a comprehensive physical exam. I concluded that her condition was not due to liver failure but that she had an abdominal tumor, probably from ovarian cancer, and that she needed to be seen by a surgical oncologist. The attending internist, the commander (also an internist), and the surgeon who was working with the commander outside of my oversight all thought that I was wrong and refused to change their opinion and her treatment. They rejected my recommendation that she be transferred immediately to a German medical center or air evacuated expeditiously back to Walter Reed Army Medical Center (WRAMC). I watched her deteriorate under their care for the next two days, at which time they had decided she was terminal. They were not going to change course. Consequently, I had a long talk with her husband, telling him that I was absolutely certain that they were wrong. The next day being Friday, I was going to declare her case to be an emergency at the end of the day and would arrange for her immediate evacuation to WRAMC and personally accompany her as a medical attendant before the commander could find out and stop me. He appreciated both my candor and my plan. The trip to WRAMC was one of the most difficult that I had encountered in my experience as a flight surgeon caring for critically ill patients being evacuated by air. Not only was she unstable in the air, but we were diverted to McGuire Air Force Base in New Jersey, where I had to admit her to the intensive care unit at Fort Dix Army Hospital and stabilize her overnight before proceeding to WRAMC the following day. She arrived at WRAMC in satisfactory condition, and I turned her over to the surgical staff. I asked them to give me updates and status reports so that I could defend my actions when I returned.

Upon my return, I reported to the commander, who told me that he was relieving me of my duties as a general surgeon and Chief of Surgery, and he was referring me for a hearing to revoke my credentials. I suggested to him that he first read the report that I brought with me from WRAMC regarding this patient and that he review the information that I had received from them on my return, all of which confirmed that I was correct in my diagnosis and prognosis and that she certainly would have died prematurely had I not acted as I did. I suggested that the substandard care which he had fostered would not result in any sanctions against me but would instead place the command in a most unfavorable light—and since this was a family member, would result in a substantial financial liability for the Army. He wisely backed off.

Later I heard from her husband, who thanked me for my efforts on her behalf and let me know that although she had undergone surgery and postoperative therapy she had lived for only about another six months. This had been precious time, however, for the two of them and their family to come to grips with her disease.

A few weeks later, the surgeon whom he had asked to observe me suddenly passed away at home. Since he lived near me, I was called to the scene after he had CPR for over 30 minutes, and he was completely unresponsive. It turns out that, unknown to me and the other surgeons, he had had a previous coronary bypass with unstable angina and this was being managed quietly by the commander.

After this, there was, for want of a better term, "an armed truce" between the commander and myself, and I enjoyed a busy surgical practice. Over time we received two new general surgeons, Dr. David Crandall, who had alternated between being either on active duty with the Army or operating in a missionary hospital in Africa for the past ten years and had a wealth of talent and experience, and Dr. Tony LaPorta, another highly skilled and brilliant academic surgeon. All of us and our families became great friends. Our daughter Laura was born that November, and we had great hopes that things would settle down.

The next crisis came just weeks later when the Deputy Commander for Clinical Services (DCCS) (a colonel charged with leadership of the clinical staff including all physicians and nurses) received unanticipated orders for Hawaii. The commander announced this at the monthly staff meeting along with the announcement that Colonel Gerald Stelter, an older, top-notch primary care physician who had returned to active duty to practice and lead primary care activities but had no interest in senior leadership beyond primary care, would be the new DCCS, which was fine with me. Unfortunately, Colonel Stelter's response was to declare loudly, "Like hell I will," and storm out of the room, with both the announcement and the reaction catching us all by surprise. The meeting broke up, and the commander called me aside to inform me that he would not even consider me for that position and would rather leave the position vacant and do without a DCCS, which was actually quite fine with me, too. Unfortunately, the CG 7th MEDCOM and the Army Surgeon General both told him that I was to assume that position. The commander called me from about 100 feet down the hall to tell me that I was going to be the new DCCS. This precipitated yet another crisis.

Prior to the departure of the previous DCCS, a position for a Quality Improvement Coordinator under the DCCS had been posted for the requisite time under civil service rules and there were three candidates, so a board was established to review the candidates' files and interview each. I replaced my predecessor as chair of the board, and we ranked the three but determined none were really suitable for the position. The commander was livid with the results, as the candidate ranked the lowest was a personal friend. He ordered me to change the board results and hire that individual. I refused to do so but reminded him that he had the authority to do the hiring in the first place, and it was his prerogative to reject the board results and hire the individual himself. I would not change the board results, however, as that would be fraud, and it would be unlawful for him to order me to do so. He then offered the position to his friend, which would have been acceptable, but he allowed the perception to spread to the staff that this was the choice of the board. I considered this action as discrediting my integrity and would undermine my moral authority to lead so I attempted to have it corrected, but when he took no action to correct this, I contacted the CG 7th MEDCOM and let him know that I could not in good conscience continue in my position under these circumstances and asked to step down and revert to clinical surgery. The result was an inspector general investigation. The hiring was judged legal as I had indicated, but it was made clear that this was not the board's decision and that I did not arbitrarily overturn the board. The IG inspection also resulted in the exposure of other problems within the organization which needed correction. The CG 7th MEDCOM contacted me and declined my request to step down and pointed out that I had been assigned to my position for a reason. Fortunately, the commander was due to rotate back to the United States and departed not too long thereafter for Fort Sam Houston, in San Antonio, Texas. My efficiency rating was reviewed by the CG 7th MEDCOM to make sure that no derogatory or punitive action was taken against me by the outgoing commander as he departed, and I remained in my position as DCCS.

Shortly after the new commander, Colonel Jack Saglio, took over, he sat down with me and Colonel Bobby Watson, the Deputy Commander for Administration (DCA), who was also hand-picked for his position, to understand why there was so much animosity and discord and why the two of us appeared to detest each other and could not work together. It became obvious in our discussion that the previous commander would give Col. Watson and me conflicting guidance. This is a leadership technique that has been used by various civilian and military senior leaders in the past. If it works, it sometimes produces a better product. However, it is more frequently a destructive technique that can be extremely divisive. As career Army officers, both of us had tried to resolve the differences with logic but it really never occurred to either of us to invoke the name of the prior commander to win the argument nor that we were being pitted against each other. This generated a sense of whiplash for the staff that resulted in divided loyalties, discord, poor morale, stress in many families, and political intrigue with malicious, truly self-serving behaviors within the staff. Once we realized what the past commander had been up to, we didn't need to be told to fix it. Within short order, Bobby and I became good friends, made it clear to the staff that there was no longer any seam between the two of us to exploit, and began the process to heal the mental wounds inflicted by the unnecessary discord and get everyone back to what we were there for—providing high-quality care to the soldiers and families we served.

Freed from the intrigue and discord, Ann was able to provide volunteer services through the American Red Cross and became the Chairman of Volunteers for the hospital.

I have never witnessed as stark a contrast as I saw between the first and second years in Augsburg, and it was 100% a reflection on the leadership before and after the change. The environment caused by toxic leadership and the impact that it had on good people committed to service to their community was a lesson that I will never forget. As with the other examples, I kept this in mind through subsequent commands or leadership positions in progressively larger organizations in assessing the climate of an organization and the performance of the leaders. The clear message to aspiring leaders is that how one leads impacts the lives of others and the productivity of the organization.

One of the highlights of serving in Europe was the ability to work in partnership with other NATO allies. I had the opportunity to participate as a 7th MEDCOM representative general surgeon in an exercise called "Operation Danish Bacon." It was common in Europe during the Cold War for NATO forces to hide field hospitals within a village building, and this exercise used a school outside of Copenhagen. This gave me the opportunity to view their techniques, and in doing so learn lessons for future use and to get to know the medical staff, most of whom spoke fluent English. I spent some time with one of the host surgeons and was surprised when he told me that he loved being in the reserve because during the week he drove a taxi in Copenhagen, which paid more than he would earn in practice; during his active duty reserve periods, he actually got to practice surgery.

As an additional duty while at the 34th General Hospital, the DCCS was also the contingency commander of the 128th Combat Support Hospital, a 200-bed mobile hospital that was minimally staffed in peacetime but maintained the vehicles and equipment in operational order in case combat was to break out in Western Europe. With my field experience, I enjoyed working closely with LTC Willie Boyd, the peacetime commander, and Major Rosemary Robinson, the peacetime chief nurse, to assist in their training and preparation. These two officers were absolutely magnificent in their meticulous planning, coordination, and execution for a winter REFORGER exercise in which we were fully staffed, drawing the clinical professional staff from the hospitals in Germany and the continental United States to co-occupy a *Bundeswehr Krankenhaus* (German military hospital) for the exercise, providing actual hospital care to soldiers with illnesses and injuries. On the wards, German and American soldiers were mixed, but the German nurses cared for the German soldiers and the American nurses cared for the American soldiers. In the operating room, if the patient was an American soldier, the surgeon and anesthesiologist were Americans assisted by German surgeons and anesthesiologists, and vice versa. In addition, we staffed and operated an ambulance train that collected real and simulated patients and transported them to military medical facilities. The train was fully equipped with an operating room and wards, but we did not provide actual surgery on the train.

As my second year in Augsburg was coming to a close, I had been selected for and was headed to the Army War College, the premier education program for senior leaders and virtually a requirement for promotion beyond colonel. Having completed a four-year tour in Germany, it seemed unlikely that we would return afterward. Therefore, we had sold or given away all of our customized furnishings for military housing in Germany (the floor plans of which were identical or mirror images in all communities) such as curtains and transformers. We purchased a new Volvo station wagon (which we picked up at the factory in Sweden) and were planning to return to the United Sates with an ocean voyage. However, on a Friday evening, with our packers due to arrive first thing Monday morning, I received a call from the CG 7th MEDCOM asking if I had shipped my household goods yet. When I told him that I had not, he asked if I would be willing to transfer to the 98th General Hospital in Nuremberg to take command of the hospital and the MEDDAC. I responded that this was my dream assignment and I would be delighted to do so. He told me, in that case, I would assume command on July 15.

The 98th General Hospital was a 1,000-bed full-service contingency hospital operating 225 beds in a fixed facility and serving a population of 75,000 active and retired military members and their families in a geographic area covering 12,000 square miles adjacent to the East German and Czechoslovakian borders. It also operated ten outlying primary care health clinics and six veterinary and preventive medicine detachments. Total staff included 1,150 people and the budget was in excess of $16,500,000. The commander had the additional duty of installation commander (similar to mayor) for Standort-Lazarett Kaserne with the hospital and dental activity compound and 154 military family housing units. The commander also was both the special court-martial convening authority for soldiers and the civilian misconduct authority for military family members and Department of Defense civilians.

There is a formal ceremony for the assumption of command, including passing of the colors from the outgoing commander to the commanding general and on to the incoming commander, followed by speeches from all three, preferably in both English and German. (Fortunately, Gary and Barbara Kindred were with us in Nuremberg and, as before, Barbara prepared me well for the German portion of my speech.)

MG Ledford's personal comments to me were brief. He emphasized his confidence in me, told me he knew I would do a great job, and advised me to call him if I needed help or additional guidance. I was honored by his expression of confidence and the freedom to act.

In his prepared remarks, MG Ledford praised my predecessor Colonel Robert Claypool for the high-quality care and great community relations that marked his tenure as commander. In return, COL Claypool thanked MG Ledford for his support, thanked the military and civilian staff for their support, and praised them for their accomplishments. He welcomed me and introduced me to the community as a strong leader and highly regarded clinician. He asked them to give me the same support that they had provided to him.

For my remarks, I thanked COL Claypool for the high standards that he had set and maintained, and I praised him and the staff for the great, well-deserved reputation in U.S. Army Europe. I thanked MG Ledford for his trust and confidence, particularly in selecting me for this command. I assured him that I would live up to or exceed his expectations. I then addressed the staff and after again praising them for their great reputation, I mapped out the future into which I wished to lead them, building upon what they had already accomplished so well. I emphasized that my primary goals in addition to top-quality health services were to build upon the current state of military readiness in the event any of us were called to support combat operations, and to sustain or create a climate where the clinical staff could practice their professions to the fullest extent, enjoy their lives and the lives of their families, and contribute to the community. At the same time, I reminded all that even though our patients really did not have a choice in where they received care, it was my intent that we would be the facility and team that they would choose if given a choice. In what can only be thought of as a prescient inspiration, I also introduced my intent to make it a requirement that every assigned active duty officer and enlisted soldier spend at least five days with one of the many combat arms maneuver units or field clinical facilities in USAREUR. This was not a USAREUR or MEDCOM policy, and I was the only medical commander to establish this requirement. It turned out to have been a tremendous help to those who were deployed to Saudi Arabia for Operations Desert Shield and Desert Storm three years later.

I realized that the leaders whom I held in the highest regard had always "walked the talk." Their behavior epitomized how they wanted others to behave. In many ways, I reflected on Colonel Paul Vanderploog from the 3d ID DISCOM, and much of what I asked of the staff in Nuremberg reflected his guidance to me. For all current and newly assigned leaders, I focused first on the essentials. I expected absolute integrity, sound ethics, competency in assigned tasks, honest and forthright responses, a bias for positive action, teamwork over individual focus, and consistency.

One of the first things that I did in command was identical to what I had done as a platoon leader, company commander, and battalion commander, but with the degree of freedom that I was granted here, this took on a different dimension. I not only looked at everything for familiarity but also with an eye to how could I improve on what was already a great organization. With my administrative and clinical deputies and often accompanied by my wife, I walked everywhere that was under my responsibility and control and talked to the organization's soldiers, leaders, and civilians. We also talked to patients in the clinics and on the wards.

One of the "VDPisms" is that an organization that looks sharp probably is a great organization until it demonstrates it is not, while one that does not look sharp is presumed not to be great until proven otherwise. As I traveled through different functional areas I took note of those that did not look as sharp as I desired. I also became aware that the span of control for the DCCS was excessive, with fourteen separate departments based on function and ten primary care clinics based upon geographic locations. I also noted that many physicians and nurses involved in direct patient care were wearing the woodland camouflage uniform (Battle Dress Uniforms otherwise known as BDUs), which neither concealed them on a hospital ward or in an office, nor gave the crisp, clean appearance I was seeking, particularly what you would expect (in those times) in a civilian facility or private practice. An observer could not tell if these uniforms were clean or had been worn for several days. The combat boots left marks on the floors and amplified footsteps, which would wake up patients taking naps in the afternoon or sleeping in the middle of the night.

I made it clear from the outset that I wanted this facility to be the type of place that our beneficiaries would want to go to if they had the choice between us and civilian facilities. I wanted to compete for patients, even if they did not actually have a choice. This proved successful beyond my expectations, as by the end of my two-year tour, we were drawing patients from the geographic regions of other Army Community Hospitals and the two medical centers in Frankfurt and Landstuhl. Emphasis was placed on quality, appearance, and courtesy. Following this initial review, I took several steps. First, all direct-patient-contact staff were to switch to uniforms comparable to what would be their normal attire in a first-class civilian facility (whites for nurses and direct-contact therapists) and green service uniforms with white coats for physicians. Following the practice of my mentor, LTG Bernie Mittemeyer, as a general surgeon commanding a hospital, I had a half-day clinic every week and performed about fifty major surgeries per year. In doing so, I could maintain clinical competence and see and hear what was really going on in the clinics, wards, and operating room. It also helped keep folks alert, knowing that I may show up in the middle of the night to perform an appendectomy or assist on a trauma case. I also was able to set the example for professional appearance when engaged in direct patient care by wearing my green uniform with a tie and white coat when in the hospital in a clinical capacity and changing to BDUs when involved in nonclinical activities.

The second step was to form an internal organizational effectiveness team to assess the lines of authority and the communication structure within the organization and to thoroughly research the actual extent of my authority to make organizational changes (which took longer than I liked, but confirmed the freedom of action that I anticipated) and then act within the full extent of that authority. The first change was to create a provisional Clinic Command that would report to the DCCS, encompassing all of the outlying clinics so that those ten organizations would report to a single leader (physician) with a deputy (nurse) who were focused on ensuring that they obtained robust support from the clinical specialists, had the resources they needed, and could achieve a high level of performance. We also created a provisional troop command led by the Deputy Commander for Administration (DCA) so that disciplinary punitive or administrative measures, if needed, could be addressed and potentially completed below the hospital commander as the special court-martial convening authority. This enhanced lines of communication between junior and senior leaders pushing decision-making down to leaders responsible and accountable for both the support and delivery of health services.

Third, there were a number of patient-unfriendly issues that could be resolved without difficulty. For example, in the obstetrics waiting area there were a number of women late in their pregnancies trying to fit into molded, rigid, and very uncomfortable plastic chairs, yet no one had taken ownership to fix this. To correct this, a patient representative was identified and given direct access to me and both of the deputy commanders for prompt problem resolution of clinical and structural or administrative issues or barriers. The 98th General Hospital became one of the most user-friendly facilities in 7th MEDCOM, if not the most user friendly.

Given the size of the hospital and the outlying clinics, painting and preventive maintenance were continuous to maintain a functional facility with a crisp appearance. Likewise, when I first arrived, emphasis on energy conservation, while laudable at a certain level, had become excessive. Multiple lights along corridors had been removed, leaving a dark and dingy appearance and leaving passageways in some areas unsafe at night. Sufficient lighting was restored to give a crisp appearance and maintain safety.

During my first year in command, Colonel Jim Eason, the Deputy Commander for Administration (DCA), approached me with an opportunity. The Department of Defense (DOD) was developing an electronic medical record, the Composite Health Care System (CHCS), and had been alpha testing the system in the military hospitals in the United States. They were then planning to move to beta testing on a worldwide basis across DOD. He thought it would be a great opportunity for us at the 98th General Hospital to get ahead of the power curve with electronic medical records and contribute to the design, impacting the future for Army Medicine. What he asked me to do was take a brief trip back to Washington DC and do some discreet but intense lobbying. I pointed out that I had no familiarity at the time with either lobbying or automated records systems, but his reply was not to worry, as he would coach me.

He did it so well that we were selected as the large overseas community hospital, beating out a couple of Army hospitals as well as Navy and Air Force facilities.

After the first year, Colonel Eason was replaced by Colonel Paul Brooke, who shortly afterward approached me on the same subject. He pointed out the complexity of the system, the need for continuous training with system upgrades, the lack of facilities within or proximate to the hospital and clinics, and the need to train the large number of staff currently in place and for ongoing training, taking into consideration both that essentially one-third of the staff rotated in and out each year and that there would be constant refinements going forward, as major improvements and modifications were to be anticipated. His proposed solution was contracting with a German company to build a training building in front of the building and then use a large crane to lift it over the front and place it in an enclosed courtyard between the forward and middle sections of the facility. The cost of all of this was just under the legal limits of my authority, and any accidents or cost overruns would likely impact me unfavorably (to say the least).

The benefit was the ability to maintain hospital efficiency while training staff, retraining staff, and implementing the new electronic medical record system for the entire DOD while we helped shape the system. The risks were cost overruns which would exceed my authority and major structural damage if the crane failed and the prefabricated building was dropped on the hospital. However, there were not any good options to maintain efficiency and productivity without potential disruption of services. Locating the training sufficiently close to the hospital wards, intensive care unit, and clinics would allow for the training of the physicians, nurses, and supporting staff without inhibiting the ability to respond to emergencies.

I concluded that I should authorize the project, as the decision was within the scope of my authority; the risk, though real, was not excessive; the company had a great reputation and insurance; the project was worth the effort; and the probability of success was sufficient to warrant the attempt. I also concluded that since I had the authority, there was no other reason to seek higher position than a feeble attempt at self-preservation. So, recalling COL Vanderploog's distinction between gambling and risk taking at an acceptable level, I chose not to pass the risk to my higher commander simply so that he would have to share the blame.

As noted, the authority to carry this out was within the upper limits of my authority and the decision was mine. I also recalled the VDPism that stated that I must know the extent of my authority and be prepared to act to the full extent of that authority. I did write a letter assuming full responsibility for what transpired, absolving any and all of my staff for the execution, and offering my immediate retirement.

Fortunately, this was successful, as was the beta test for the system, which, with regular modifications including those that we suggested as well as multiple modifications since then, is still in use today, enhancing the efficiency of military medicine. To this day, I look back at this as one of the high points of my career. It certainly enhanced my reputation in military medicine at the time, yet I also still credit Colonels Eason and Brooke for that success every chance I get.

Another initiative previously noted which provided great dividends later was to establish the requirement for all military medical staff to spend at least one week in the field each year with one of the line medical units. I turned this over to the Chief of Plans, Operations, and Training, Major Gary Kindred, to accomplish. His staff tracked all field exercises in Germany and worked with the 98th General Hospital staff to arrange for training opportunities and to make sure that the requirement could be met by all. There was some grumbling at the time, as this was not a 7th Medical Command requirement and many did not share my enthusiasm for field operations, but I considered it essential for readiness of the field units and of the potential professional staff that would be required should a contingency requirement occur. At the time I considered this to be a long-term investment and never dreamed it would provide so much value so quickly. This was to prove tremendously beneficial, as two to three years later many of these people were deployed for Desert Shield and Desert Storm. I encountered several of my former staff members in the desert, and they were all now very appreciative of their field training in Europe.

I also found that with over 1,100 staff members, it was no longer possible to get to know all on a personal basis and to make sure everyone understood and followed my guidance. For all newly assigned officers and NCOs, I would either personally or in groups go over my command philosophy and guidance, and I would have a semiannual newcomers' briefing for all as well as open-forum periodic updates. Two things became clear to me: first, I could not see everything and had to trust my leaders down the chain of command to communicate my guidance and execute our mission, and, second, I had to do spot checks to verify. In this, I was assisted by a tremendous staff and an outstanding NCO, CSM Lawrence Williams, who seemed to be everywhere.

Our time in Nuremberg was particularly gratifying for Ann. Her mother had joined us for this tour and, in addition to being a fantastic cook, she was able to watch over the children while Ann increased her volunteer responsibilities with the American Red Cross. She became the Region III Chairman covering Bavaria, Turkey, and Greece, and was a Maternal Child Nurse Consultant for Europe with a relative rank of colonel.

Two years passed too quickly, and it seemed no time at all before I was back on the parade field relinquishing the colors to MG Tom Travis to pass on to my successor. In my remarks I reflected upon what I had asked of everyone when I assumed command and let them know that not only did they all accomplish everything I asked of them, they actually exceeded my expectations with distinction. During these two years, we had developed a reputation that resulted in a significant number of soldiers and their families voting for us with their feet: rather than going to their community hospitals, they were driving the extra miles and two to three hours on the road to have their health needs met at the 98th General Hospital. We had become the hospital they chose even though they had the choice to obtain care closer to home. Based in great part upon the rating of the 98th General Hospital, the Nuremberg Military Community received the award for the "overseas Large Community of Excellence." Ann and I could not be prouder of the role we played.

We departed for Carlisle Barracks, Pennsylvania, to attend the Army War College as was intended two years before. This time, we did not get a last-minute change of plans. We sadly left Germany, expecting that after six years there, we would not be offered the opportunity to return.

We settled in to academic life quickly. I was part of a seminar group which included lieutenant colonels and colonels from a variety of branches in the Army with no two from the same branch: a young executive from the U.S. Forest Service; a brigadier general in the Egyptian Army; and three faculty advisors from the Army, Navy, and State Department.

We shared ideas, had an exciting social life, and settled into American life. The course work was rigorous but not excessive. The group studied the budgetary process and funding cycle for the DOD with emphasis on the Army, and there was considerable emphasis on the definition of a true vital national interest and the military strategies designed to protect those interests. There was a writing requirement which could be filled individually or in a group paper. I worked across seminar groups with other Medical Corps Officers—Colonels Thomas Clements, Vernon Spaulding, and Stephen Xenakis—to produce a futuristic vision for military medicine entitled "Army Medical Department 2005," for which we received a Distinguished Essay Award from the Chairman of the Joint Chiefs of Staff (General Colin Powell). Many of our projections proved accurate and helped shape the future.

The academic highlight of the year was the final campaign simulation in which Iran had attacked Kuwait through Basra, Iraq, and the United States was leading a campaign to push them back. This was fortuitously similar to the invasion of Kuwait by Iraq months later. As the Medical Corps officer, my role was to plan the template for the medical support. This was similar, but on a far more expansive scale, to what I accomplished in the Canal Zone as a young major. The research that I had to do for my role in this planning and the vision from the logistics team in terms of movement of people and equipment and battle space management from the operations team proved to be of tremendous help in my next assignment when VII Corps was called to deploy to Iraq for Operations Desert Shield and Storm.

This year was an easy time for Ann and me, but it was more difficult than expected for our children, who were born and raised in Germany. In Germany, we received only one English-language channel: the Armed Forces Network. The advertising was limited to operational security and public service ads about not drinking and driving, use of seatbelts, fitness issues, etc. The number of television channels and programs we received in Carlisle was a shock, and they were exposed to advertising for such products as sugar disguised as cereal, fast food, and all types of toys and games which we had thus far avoided. They also were used to shopping in the villages with deutsche marks and pfennigs rather than dollars and cents, and they had no concept of the value of nickels, dimes, and quarters. Parenting can be much easier without commercial advertising.

As the year at the War College was coming to a close, we were all awaiting our follow-on assignments. Medical Corps branch asked me for a preference, and I indicated that I would like to return to Germany to command one of the two Regional Medical Centers. The Chief of Medical Corps Affairs, Brigadier General Mike Scotti, let me know in very clear terms that a return to Europe was out of the question, as I had already spent too much time there. My argument to the contrary was not persuasive, and I was told that I would instead command Evans Army Community Hospital at Fort Carson in Colorado Springs. This was a great opportunity, and we thanked him for setting it up and began our preparations for a move to Colorado.

However, shortly before graduation, our friend Colonel Warren Todd called from the Medical Corps Assignments Office to tell me that Lieutenant General Fred Franks (who had commanded the 1st Armored Division which I had supported as the 98th General Hospital Commander) had rejected two slates of candidates for the position and had made a personal, by-name request that I be assigned to that position. He told me that when a senior officer at that level requested someone by name, the assignment was made unless there was an overwhelming argument to the contrary, and there was not—so Ann and I were going to (happily) return to Germany.

Toward the end of my year at the Army War College, however, I developed the disturbing symptoms of an electric shock radiating along my fingers and in my feet, as well as numbness developing in the soles of my feet. Before departing for Germany, I visited with the Neurology Service at Walter Reed Army Medical Center for an evaluation, but this was completely negative, including a test for Lyme disease. The conclusion was that I likely had a rare neurologic syndrome, likely inherited, that would likely be terminal, but not for many years. They offered to recommend that I be placed on the Temporary Disabled Retired List, but I chose to continue on to Europe instead. This proved to be another great choice, as once back in Germany, I discussed my situation with a classmate from my internship class who was an infectious-disease expert. He told me that there was a European version of Lyme disease which was different enough that it often did not show up on testing in American laboratories. He recommended that I try a two-week course of Doxycycline, which brought rapid, though short-lived, relief.

We quickly settled back into life in Germany. We were in a hotel in town for several days before moving into our quarters and while we were there, we witnessed the daytime and nighttime celebrations when Germany won the World Cup, which, as avid soccer fans, we would have enjoyed a whole lot more had we not just arrived and had a bad case of jet lag, made worse by three little children with bad jet lag, too. Still, we quickly reconnected with all of our friends from the years before, and Ann quickly resumed her role with the American Red Cross as the Maternal Child Nurse Consultant for Europe, but she also was included in the ARC Operation Desert Storm Planning Council.

Shortly after I arrived back in Germany, the Iraqi Army invaded Kuwait. A few days later, I was attending a 3d Infantry Division (3ID) Headquarters exercise and sitting in a tent talking to LTG Franks when the 3ID CG, Major General Wilson (Dutch) Shoffner, came into the tent and started to talk with LTG Franks about the invasion and the U.S. response. Realizing that 3d Army (the Army component of Central Command or ARCENT) and the XVIII Airborne Corps were deploying to defend Saudi Arabia and knowing that another Corps would be required for driving the Iraqi Army out of Kuwait, LTG Franks pulled out a world map and pointed out to MG Shoffner that VII Corps could get to Kuwait faster than III Corps could even completely get out of Fort Hood, Texas. Since I already had been briefed that VII Corps was to be inactivated within the next year, I immediately concluded that this was a real possibility and I should certainly not mention or discuss this conversation with anyone. However, I was not surprised when early that November, it was announced on Armed Forces Radio and Television that VII Corps would be deploying to Saudi Arabia. What I did not know was that initial planning was already underway at Kelley Barracks in Germany in a top-secret planning cell to which I was added shortly thereafter to begin planning the medical support.

In preparation for deployment, the primary and special staff began daily morning and evening meetings with the Chief of Staff and CG. Deployment of the Corps would pull units from all over Germany, and most heavy vehicles and equipment and some people would go by sea while the others would go by air. This required coordinating the requirements involved in moving people and equipment from all over West Germany to sea ports and large air fields, particularly Rhine Main and

Ramstein.

The deployment to the sea and ports for heavy equipment and vehicles was primarily by rail or barge and required bracing the equipment with heavy lumber to avoid damage. Some tracked vehicles and heavy equipment containers also were moved on special tractor trailer trucks designed for this purpose and were to be transported to Saudi Arabia, as well. Many of the tracked vehicles (tanks, armored fighting vehicles, and armored personnel carriers) were transported to the ports by rail. Other heavy equipment was transported by barge on the rivers and canals. Most of the people would be transported to the airports by bus.

Those of us on the Corps staff would have to individually track the people and equipment so that every item would end up in the right place at the right time to move forward in the desert, keeping the ports free for follow-on forces.

Training schedules were adjusted so that at the time of deployment, teams would be at maximum proficiency and readiness. I learned several leadership lessons in the process. First, initially when there was more time, LTG Franks was more open to lengthy discussion on planning aspects and collective evaluation of the risks and benefits of different courses of action, but as time became increasingly critical, seeking input became more controlled and decisions would be made promptly and decisively before quickly moving to the next subject. (The lesson here is that as the time frame shortens and a situation increases in urgency, the decision maker needs to act more rapidly and decisively and move on to the next issue.) Also, as operations became more imminent, LTG Franks established a "good ideas cut off point," as last-minute changes without coordination and rehearsal were more likely to decrease rather than improve the probability of success. There is a saying in the Army to the effect that a good plan brilliantly executed has a far greater chance of success than a "better" plan poorly executed.

On a personal note, during this time period, my neurologic symptoms gradually recurred and my infectious-disease classmate recommended a full month of Doxycycline, which again quickly controlled my symptoms. This was important because I was responsible for the extensive medical preparation for the deploying force and I was determined to fulfill my role as the VII Corps Surgeon.

The Army was transitioning from the old inflatable hospitals (MUSTs) to modern lightweight tents and expandable containers (DEPMEDS) for operating room, radiology, laboratory, etc. Initial or refresher training was needed for all medical personnel to be prepared to handle chemical and biological warfare casualties, so a team was sent from Fort Detrick, and every deploying Medical Department officer received this training before deployment. Training on the DEPMEDS systems was initiated, and it was discovered that most of the sets were being "shipped short" with a list of additional items needed that was unique for each set. Initial estimates for potential casualties were over 10,000, and there was a critical need for ventilators for deploying hospitals.

To facilitate my planning role, I took two pre-deployment trips to Saudi Arabia to meet with the leaders of the evolving medical structure, including the medical leadership of 3d Army and the XVIII Airborne Corps. I also toured the port for arriving equipment. Two things were quickly obvious. First, the amount and type of equipment arriving made it obvious to me that unless Iraq backed down, we were going to fight. Second, there were many individuals with other agendas besides simply defeating the enemy. It appeared that although the numbers involved were not substantial, there were still too many leaders who planned to use this as an opportunity to advance their own personal agenda, or parochial interests and careers. This became increasingly obvious as I learned that the total force was going to be composed of Regular Army, Army Reserve, and Army National Guard. I was disappointed to find that some in the Regular Army were dismissive of the "weekend warriors" in the Guard and Reserve, but also found that National Guard and Army Reserve units were not particularly fond of each other, as in peacetime they competed for status and resources.

The first problem this caused for those of us in VII Corps was a decision at 3d Army, the Army component of Central Command (ARCENT), to create and stand up a Medical Command (3d MEDCOM) instead of utilizing the 332 Medical Brigade that was specifically designed and trained to manage Theatre Army health services, and had already been given activation orders. As a consequence, the 213th Medical Brigade (MED BDE) was not activated even though this brigade was staffed and trained for Corps-level support and for years had been specifically designated for and trained with VII Corps. The Regular Army Medical Group (30th MED GP) in VII Corps had actually just completed a training exercise with the 213 MED BDE at Camp Shelby, Mississippi, in September. The difference is that (in increasing order of size and sophistication) the Corps-level hospitals are Mobile Army Surgical Hospitals (MASH–80 beds), Combat Support Hospitals (CSH–200 beds), and Evacuation Hospitals (EVAC–400 beds) have varying degrees of mobility, and follow the flow of battle, while Theatre Army Hospitals are generally of 1,000 beds or more (Field Hospitals, Station Hospitals, and Hospital Centers) and tend not to move and may be established in fixed facilities. The differences in leadership requirements and support are substantial.

I arrived back in Germany from my second visit to Saudi Arabia on December 20 and deployed with the Corps Headquarters on December 26. At least I was home for Christmas and spent the majority of the night with my wife, assembling a complicated doll house for my two daughters and seeing their smiles in the morning. These are the moments that sustain soldiers.

Shortly after I arrived back in Saudi Arabia, I met with BG Michael Strong, CG 332 MED BDE, and his Chief of Staff, Colonel Paul Holland, and we spent an evening discussing the situation. They were very straight forward in acknowledging that their staff did not have the depth of training and talent for their newly designated role and they likely did not have the time to develop it. Together we developed a solution that we would merge the 30th Medical Group headquarters with the 332 Medical Brigade headquarters under BG Strong's leadership, placing the best-trained people in each of the critical positions and dividing responsibility for leadership and execution to COL Jesse Fulfer (Cdr 30th MED GP), who would assume the role of Deputy Commander for Operations and provide leadership to, planning for, and coordination of the two medical groups which would directly support the combat divisions. I would serve as Deputy Commander for Support and perform the same functions for the larger hospitals, the air ambulance battalion, the ground ambulance battalion, and the medical logistics battalion as well as the multiple detachments (Dental, Mental Health, Preventive Medicine, etc.). BG Strong as CG 332 Medical Brigade would also assume my position as the Corps Surgeon, providing input directly to the Corps Chief of Staff and as the Brigade Commander although I remained on LTG Franks's personal staff and would maintain direct access to the Chief of Staff and Corps Commander if needed. I briefed this proposal to BG Landry, the Corps Chief of Staff, and then to LTG Franks, who concurred and approved the reorganization.

This proved effective, but there were other issues to deal with. When one of the assigned MASHs reported to its mobilization station, it was discovered that greater than 50% of the staff were not qualified in their assigned positions. Soldiers from another MASH in a different city were called to active service to round out the staffing. Unfortunately, when they arrived in Saudi Arabia, it was also discovered that neither unit had the requisite military training or equipment. The solution was to form a MASH-like hospital out of the Regular Army 31st CSH, utilizing vehicles and equipment from both organizations to create what we called a super CSH/MASH with a MASH light component able to move forward to support a division.

Because of the problems with fielding DEPMEDS in a combat environment, particularly with the finding that they were facing undeterminable shortages due to the ship-short policy, upon my recommendation in the Kelly Barracks planning cell, we made the decision early on to pair the larger hospitals along Tapline Road so that they could share resources and evenly distribute patients. As logical as this sounded, this proved to be another area in which obtaining cooperation between units was problematic. For example, one pairing of hospitals (one Army Reserve the other Army National Guard and one from the south and one from the north) had one hospital without a mobile kitchen unit (misappropriated by another unit in the port) but with plenty of heaters for their tents, while the other had no heaters for their tents but had a fully equipped kitchen. When I visited the two hospitals, I discovered that despite January temperatures in the 20s and 30s in the desert, instead of sharing resources, one was warm and eating field rations and the other was freezing but eating cooked meals. Upon discovering this, I admonished both commanders and told them I would return the next day and if this was not fixed they should have their bags packed, as I would remove them from command and they would leave with me on the helicopter. When I returned the next day, both hospitals were being fed properly and the heaters were redistributed, but the receiving hospital commander was refusing to allow his soldiers to use them because they were worried about being harassed that "they wouldn't be clean enough" when they returned them. I gave that commander an hour to get every heater fired up or turn over his command to his deputy and meet me at the helicopter. He got them lit, but this was the sort of pettiness that I found intolerable as we were preparing for war. After this episode, I was able to bring my West Point classmate COL Reggie Moore over from the XVIII Airborne Corps to assist me and to form "Task Force Evac," which would oversee the larger hospitals and allow me focus on the air and ground evacuation system and establish and provide senior leadership to the logistical support required for the entire brigade.

During this period, my neurologic symptoms again recurred, so I met with an infectious-disease physician deployed with one of the hospitals in VII Corps. He agreed with the treatment that I had received but recommended that we try an additional three months of Doxycycline along with a course of steroids. Again, my symptoms rapidly abated, but the side effect was a great sensitivity to sunlight, causing a rapid chemical sunburn with limited exposure. Fortunately, I could wear my aviation gloves at all times and, with the assistance of the VII Corps Chief of Staff, I was able to minimize (but not eliminate) my sun exposure.

By the time the Desert Storm ground war commenced under BG Strong's sound leadership and ability to bring people together, COL Fulfer and I finally had the medical support system organized with everyone focused and pulling together on our mission to handle the massive casualties projected and provide the high-quality support that soldiers deserve in a combat environment. To our relief, the casualty numbers were far fewer than predicted, but we were prepared. From a leadership perspective, I had to employ every tool that I had learned, from my time at West Point up to that day.

After VII Corps returned to Germany, the deactivation announcement for VII Corps was made. Over the following years, military communities were to be reduced in size or closed and units were to be either transferred to V Corps or inactivated. I was offered command of the USAREUR contingency hospital with assurances that this would lead to my early promotion to brigadier general. However, this would mean that I would be away from home much of the time and that there was a distinct possibility that I would end up deploying with that hospital. I discussed this with my boss, the VII Corps Chief of Staff who had spoken to the Commanding General of the 7th Medical Command, and he encouraged me to take the position and cautioned me that this was a once-in-a-lifetime opportunity.

The deployment clearly had an impact on the family. Several of the senior officers' wives returned to the United States during this period, and none of the other families had children as young as ours. Ann had to have hand surgery and was pretty much fending for herself with children three, five, and seven when I departed for Saudi Arabia. Our son, Tom, the youngest, had a child-size "Battle Dress Uniform" which he wore constantly (except when off the Kaserne) when I departed and every day until well after I returned. When I returned, our children had been through an emotionally intense six months due to my absence and the increased threat from terrorists directed at military families deployed for the Gulf War. Our housing area was surrounded by German police on horseback outside the wire and automatic weapons positions within the wire. There were demonstrators constantly at the gate with "No blood for oil" signs in English and German. The girls, Carolyn and Laura, attended the International School of Stuttgart in the nearby village of Moehringen. Ann had to drive them to school in the morning, park the car and walk a block or two to the school (which now had an armed guard at the entrance), walk back to the car, look under the car for bombs, and then drive back to the gate. Due to the protestors and the requirement for the Military Police to check every car for bombs, it took up to half an hour just to enter the Kaserne. Circumstances were not too different for my wife and children than they were for my family when I was a seven-year-old child in Trieste. An amusing incident (in retrospect) came during the deployment when my wife realized the girls had left the house and she ran out of the house to look for them. Almost immediately a Military Police car with blue lights flashing pulled up and the Military Policewoman asked my wife what was wrong. When Ann told her the girls were missing, she climbed on her car to look around and then asked if one had been wearing a pink jacket. One of them was, and the two girls were spotted bringing Girl Scout cookies to the soldiers at the machine gun position defending our neighborhood. Another similar incident occurred one night when the oldest, who was learning about the stars in school, went out front to look at the sky without telling her mother. When Ann heard voices in the front yard and saw that Carolyn was not in the house, she rushed out to look for her and found her talking to a Military Policeman who had spotted her flashlight and was talking to her as he walked her to the door.

After discussing the potential assignment with Ann, I chose to decline the offer for command of the contingency hospital. Ann and I felt strongly that the family needed me more as a husband and father than the Army did as a general so I declined the offer.

We took advantage of the slower pace and the ability to travel. This also allowed the children to remain in the same school for a second full year, during which Ann served as the President of the Board of Directors for the International School. We took the children with us to visit Denmark, Belgium, England, and France, including standing on the Normandy beaches at 6:00 a.m. at low tide in early June, where we could vividly see the remaining rusted hulks from World War II and picture our VII Corps soldiers of an earlier day charging ashore against fierce opposition. This was followed by a visit to the American Cemetery, with its immaculate appearance and row upon row of tombstones. I cannot adequately describe the emotional impact this memory generated for all of us. Later, we also had the opportunity to drive across what had been a border representing the "Iron Curtain," which we were prohibited from even approaching except with elements of the 2d ACG escorting us. We brought the children to visit Prague and East Germany, including a return visit to what had been East Berlin which was no longer divided into East and West.

Following this year, we returned to the United States where I became the commander of Keller Army Community Hospital at West Point for a two- to three-year tour. This was a prestigious position, as I was also the U.S. Military Academy Surgeon and was on the Academic Board. I was fortunate to have an internist assigned who had trained in Europe and was quite familiar with the European variant of Lyme. By then, there was more-sophisticated testing available in the United States, and I finally tested positive for Lyme, confirming the presumptive diagnosis. I was also beginning to have symptoms again and developed bilateral carpal tunnel symptoms, a common Lyme disease complication. At this point, the internist decided that since Doxycycline was a bacteriostatic antibiotic (controls but does not kill bacteria), the best course of treatment would be to insert a catheter into the large vein on the right side of my heart and administer a daily dose of Rocephin (an intravenous cephalosporin which is a bactericidal antibiotic that actually kills the bacteria) for a total of four months. With my assignment, I had to travel a fair amount, so my secretary would arrange for a hotel room with a refrigerator, the pharmacist would prepare sufficient Rocephin for up to two weeks, and I would self-administer the antibiotic each evening in my room. By the end of this assignment, I had had carpal tunnel releases in both wrists but was symptom free, with the exception of decreased sensation in my fingers and my feet, which has now been stable for twenty-five years. However, it was clear at the time that I would not be able to go back to full-time surgery, and I realized that my future was in executive medicine.

The assignment at West Point turned into another short assignment, as a great opportunity presented itself when a vacancy for a Command Surgeon became available. General Dennis Reimer, who as a colonel had been the Chief of Staff of the 8th ID when I arrived in Germany, had become the Commander of Army Forces Command (FORSCOM), commanding all combat forces stationed in the Continental United States, and he was happy to have me join his staff as the Command Surgeon.

Life at West Point, on a small, relatively isolated military installation adjacent to the small town of Highland Falls, surrounded by forests and mountains, was similar in many ways to living in military housing in Germany. It is not a typical American community with its own unique culture. Therefore, the assignment to Fort McPherson in Atlanta, for which we bought a house in Fayetteville, Georgia, was ironically analogous to when we moved to Fayetteville, Arkansas, in 1959, where my siblings and I became "Americanized" as children. Until then, our children had only been in the United States for less than one year at Carlisle, Pennsylvania, and barely one year at West Point. We drove down the East Coast, which gave our children a chance to see different American towns and cities. They became more aware of the vast difference in size and travel times between what they were used to in West Germany and the United States. (For example, when we lived in southern Bavaria, we could drive from Augsburg to Denmark in less than one day.)

We settled in Fayetteville, and the entire family became active in the community. The children attended public schools and were immersed in the culture. There was a terrific soccer program, and I was able to coach teams in the youth program. These were fun but hectic days, as on many weekends each child would be playing in a different county. The children joined either the Girl Scouts or Cub Scouts and were active in the programs. At last, we could see signs of the real Americanization of our children. Until then, whenever oldest daughter would see a program on Germany she would start to cry, saying that she "missed her homeland." We would gently remind her that the United States was her homeland and that even though she was born there, we had actually only been guests in Germany.

My duties required me to travel, visiting combat forces and medical units around the country and in Korea, but I would almost always be home for the weekend. After two years I was nominated to command the hospital at Fort Benning, Georgia, but shortly thereafter I was selected for brigadier general and was instead transferred to Fort Sam Houston, Texas, to be the Deputy Commanding General for Healthcare Operations, Chief of Medical Corps Affairs, and the Head of the Contracting Agency for the Army Medical Command.

There was a fairly extensive orientation to becoming a general officer. The first part consisted of a one-week orientation in Arlington, Virginia. There is a certain mystique that goes with being a general, but the danger in this was also stressed. You are constantly "on stage," and people will observe your conduct both on and off duty. There are special rules for general officer housing and a budget that is subject to annual congressional review. There are specific rules for use of military vehicles and aircraft and communication services, and violation of these rules has led to the downfall of many senior officers. All Army officers are under constant scrutiny by those they lead and the local community, but if is far more intense for general officers. Perceptions of impropriety or favoritism can destroy a career, particularly if there are nebulous circumstances that should have been anticipated and corrected. For every real or apparent evil deed in the world, someone always sees—and that someone is likely to tell, particularly if the deed involves a senior officer. Unfortunately, perception often is stronger than reality and can lead to unfortunate consequences if fostered.

In counseling developing leaders I have found the following tale useful to illustrate the potential danger of incorrect perceptions:

> In the rainforests of South America, there are still small tribes that have never been exposed to civilization, and the local governments have made a substantial effort to protect them from this exposure.

However, for the sake of discussion, imagine that on a cloud-covered day someone who has studied this population and learned its language floated over the village in a balloon, and in a deeply resonant voice called out in their language that he knew what they had done and he was angry. For punishment, if they did not sacrifice the first-born child in every family, he would return and destroy their village and kill every inhabitant, and render the land uninhabitable forevermore. The reality is a prankster in a balloon. Perception is the belief that this is the voice of God.

Obviously, this is hyperbole, but there are plenty of instances in which misperceptions of impropriety have ended careers. When I was the Deputy Commanding General of the Army Medical Command for Healthcare Operations, I worked for Major General Jim Peake, who pointed out that "the truth is a powerful weapon," which is great advice. Short of not allowing the perception to develop in the first place, the only good defense is an imperative to get the truth out completely, openly, and as quickly as possible. Otherwise, the perceptions will fester and continue to be believed, and even cited well into the future.

We were supposed to be at Fort Sam Houston for at least two years and likely longer, but after only one year I was transferred to Fort Gordon, Georgia, due to an unanticipated vacancy and assigned as the Commanding General of Dwight David Eisenhower Army Medical Center (DDEAMC), and Commanding General of the Southeast Regional Medical Command (SERMC) over all Army Hospitals in Alabama, Georgia, South Carolina, and Tennessee, as well as Army Health Clinics in Florida and Puerto Rico. I was simultaneously the Department of Defense TRICARE Lead Agent for Regions 3 and 15, the Southeast United States, Latin America, and Canada, and I was the active component Deputy Commanding General for 3d MEDCOM, a deployable field headquarters for contingencies in Southeast Asia, particularly Saudi Arabia and Kuwait. Fortunately, I had a separate staff for each position, but sometimes I would wake up in the morning wondering which of these positions would drive my itinerary for the day. I had 7,500 military and civilian personnel under my command and was quickly reminded of MG Ledford's approach: I would have faith in those I knew would do well and more closely manage those that I suspected might need my help until they could excel on their own. I remembered the lesson I learned in Vietnam when our battalion commander would call the company commander from his helicopter, telling him to go check out footprints in the sand from 5,000 feet in the air. The view is a whole lot different from that height.

I continued to push the envelope to the full extent of my authority in these roles. As I was responsible for costs incurred both in the military facilities and civilian hospitals through my DOD role as Lead Agent, my chief of staff, Colonel George Masi—now retired and the Chief Executive Officer of Harris Health System in Houston, Texas—led a staff study which found there were a number of patients requiring nonemergency cardiovascular surgery and other high-cost procedures who would like to be treated in the military system at DDEAMC. As one of our subordinate commands at Fort Rucker, Alabama, was the rotary-wing air ambulance unit, with a Military Assistance to Safety and Traffic (MAST) mission and the staff had identified a few small fixed-wing aircraft (C12 twin-engine propeller) with side cargo doors that were excess to the requirements of the service, we discussed the possibility of obtaining a couple of those aircraft for the air ambulance unit at Fort Rucker to use for medical transport in the region. Colonel (later Major General) David Rubenstein, the Deputy Commander for Administration for DDEAMC, and Colonel George Masi conducted a detailed analysis and prepared a proposal to do this. Pros and cons were outlined, and we staffed it through the office of the Army Surgeon General. At first, we were given a dozen reasons why we could not do this, including the fact that this was technically an Air Force mission, for which they would have to use a C9 (military version of a 767), which would have been prohibitively expensive. We responded to every argument and it took us almost a year to accomplish, but we finally obtained the approval and the aircraft. After a few months in service, the program was working smoothly, and the Air Force evacuation system, which had previously opposed the plan, even asked us to carry out some small missions for them, saving several thousand dollars with each one.

After I had been at SERMC about eighteen months, I was at a conference with the Army Surgeon General, and he advised me that I would likely leave Fort Gordon late the following year and return to Fort Sam Houston to become the Commandant of the Army Medical Department

Center and School. This would probably last for two years, and then to Washington DC. Both of these assignments were ones that I had desired for many years and for which I believed I was very well qualified. I appreciated his confidence in me and the input.

However, while I was at this conference, an executive recruiter had tried to call me but had reached my wife at home instead. They were searching for a Medicaid medical director for Blue Cross and Blue Shield of Vermont (BCBSVT), and he was a bit surprised, but pleased, when she said we would consider it. Upon my return home, we had a long discussion about our future. The projected military assignments were my dream assignments. However, they also meant that our oldest daughter would have to move as a high school senior, her younger sister would also have to move as a high school senior, and there was a good chance that their younger brother would have to do that as well. To make our dilemma worse, we had many ties to Vermont. Ann had graduated from Plattsburgh State University across Lake Champlain from Burlington, we were avid skiers, Ann's grandparents were born in Vermont, and her great-uncle had been the Commandant of Norwich University. We had always dreamed of retiring there following my military career, but we were also keenly aware that meaningful retirement jobs in Vermont were few and far between. Keeping this in mind, I interviewed for the position and Ann went up to Vermont to look around the area, after which we discussed this at length as a family. Factoring in the anticipated cost of schooling in the two environments, the travel requirements for me, and the parallel responsibilities Ann would have with my positions, we made the decision as a family for me to retire the following June. I let the Surgeon General know so that they could make alternate plans for those assignments. For me, this was painful, but for the family, it was the right thing to do.

We built a house in Waterbury Center, Vermont, and became very active in the community. We lived in the same neighborhood as my medical partner at Blue Cross, and our older two children were essentially the same age as his. Ann was elected to the School Board and also served on the board of the Senior Center. Our oldest daughter entered the tenth grade and her eleventh school. I was active with my son's Boy Scout troop, serving as the Troop Committee Chairman, and ultimately as Chairman of the Long Trail District, and Tom became an Eagle Scout.

The kids learned to ski and snowboard. There were six resorts we could get to in less than an hour and a half, and we had season passes for at least one of these resorts every year. After Ann and I transitioned to cross-country skiing, there were even more opportunities. Our favorite became the Trapp Family Lodge, which was in Stowe and only about twenty minutes from home. Life was great!

Professionally, I was exposed to an entirely different industry and, of necessity, rapidly became well versed in the intricacies of health insurance and managed care. During my second year I was nominated to the National Council of Physician Executives (NCPE) and later served as vice chairman and chairman for two years each. During this time Dr. Alan Korn, Chief Medical Officer of the Blue Cross and Blue Shield Association, expanded the NCPE from a small nominative group of about fifteen members to add the chief physician from every Blue Cross Plan and then added the chief pharmacist from each plan. By the time my term as chairman ended, membership had grown from roughly a dozen members to well over one hundred, making the meetings more difficult to manage and consensus more difficult to achieve, as there are significant vested interests between very small and very large plans and between not-for-profit and for-profit plans.

Because of my ties to Arkansas, whenever I was at the NCPE I sought out two individuals from Arkansas Blue Cross and Blue Shield: Dr. Jim Adamson, the Senior Vice President and Chief Medical Officer, and Joseph Smith, Senior Vice President and Chief Information Officer. We became friends, and I enjoyed hearing about all of the amazing changes in Arkansas following my departure in 1963.

During the summer of 2009, Nick Bacon—who had been the squad leader of my platoon in Vietnam—was diagnosed with metastatic cancer in a lymph node that was removed from his neck. He called me when the results came back and told me that they wanted to remove all of his teeth and begin radiation and chemo therapies. He told me that he had decided that, instead, he planned to live life to its fullest until he no longer could enjoy it, at which time he would go to hospice. Given the realistic prognosis and Nick's desire to lead an active life and maintain his life style until the very end, coupled with his faith and his courage, I could tell that this was a reasoned decision and fit his personality. Because he was living in Rose Bud, Arkansas, a small community north of

Little Rock, Captain Treadwell and others arranged for a mini reunion and farewell to Nick in Little Rock that September. Ann and I attended, and it was great to spend much of the time with Nick and the others and share old memories. It was an emotional event for all of us.

As we were going to be in Little Rock, and Ann had never been to Arkansas, I wanted to take the opportunity to show her the beauty of the state. After the gathering, we took time to walk around downtown Little Rock and then set off for Fayetteville in the northwestern corner of the state. We went west on Interstate 40 toward Fort Smith, and to my surprise there was an interstate highway north past Fayetteville. I was even more astonished to see a sign stating "Fayetteville Next 6 Exits." What had been a medium-sized university town was now a large city.

I drove Ann by the house where my family had lived, and we stopped to take a picture. Totally out of character for me, I went over and talked to the woman working in the yard. She and her husband had done a lot of remodeling, and they were very friendly and happy to show us around. She reminded us of the history of the house, as it had actually been moved from College Avenue to East Prospect Street not long before we lived there. Next, we went to the University of Arkansas, where we toured the campus and I showed her Peabody Hall, which had been the University High School where I graduated with twenty-one classmates. From there it was north to Eureka Springs and then east across the northern tier to Jonesboro, where we spent the night at the home of Bert and Cindy Price. Bert had worked for me twice in Europe, first as Division Psychiatrist in Bad Kreuznach and subsequently as the Chief of Psychiatry when I was the DCCS in Augsburg, and we had become good friends. He and his son, Ham, attended my promotion to brigadier general. (Ham is now a staff sergeant in the U.S. Army Band in Washington.) We enjoyed remembering our time in Europe and catching up with each other on our subsequent careers. The next day, Ann and I headed back to Vermont not having a clue that we would end up moving to Little Rock in less than a year.

At BCBSVT, we had a relatively new Chief Executive Officer who had been in that position less than a year. For reasons that I still do not comprehend, he decided to reorganize the medical services area even though the three medical directors were an unusually strong group, with solid professional reputations and highly regarded in their communities and by the practicing medical professionals in Vermont. This was his prerogative, and he chose to do so by letting the current corporate medical director go and bringing in a different physician to take his place. He had discussed this person with me beforehand, and I pointed out to him that I knew that man and was convinced that he would have difficulty with the culture in Vermont and he would not work well with any of us. I cautioned him that this was not a prudent move. However, he said that the man was highly recommended, so he ignored my input and hired him.

The incumbent left the first of February and shortly thereafter I asked Alan Korn to let the members of the NCPE know that I would be available and was willing to leave Vermont. Within five days, I had several opportunities, including two in Washington State, one in central Pennsylvania, one in Tennessee, and one in Arkansas, where I would replace Dr. Jim Adamson as the Senior Vice President and Chief Medical Officer. There was no doubt in my mind which I would prefer, and Ann had really liked Arkansas during our visit the previous fall. Within a month, I had interviewed with the Chief Executive Officer (CEO) and the Chief Operating Officer (COO), toured the Arkansas Blue Cross and Blue Shield (ABCBS) facilities, and received a formal offer which I was delighted to accept, as it felt like it was meant to be. I was headed home! I tendered my resignation and was to report the first of June.

The third medical director departed in early September. All three of us received offers for far more prestigious positions within larger and more complicated organizations (two of us became senior vice presidents for vastly larger health plans and the third become corporate medical director for managed Medicaid at a very large, prestigious plan). The physician whose hiring triggered our departures left the plan less than nine months later, and the replacements hired for myself and the original third medical director also departed within a year. The loss of this many physicians and the cost of recruitment, orientation, and training in managed care were consequences that should have been considered before the initial abrupt termination of the current corporate medical director, emphasizing the need for analyzing not just the direct impact of a critical action, but also any anticipatable second- and third-order effects of the action—a concept I had adopted over many years during my military career.

From a family perspective this was perfect timing, as our daughters had already left home. The older was then an Air Force officer in Colorado Springs, and the younger was married to an Air Force officer, and was living in Fort Collins, Colorado, while completing her doctorate in audiology. Our son was due to graduate from the University of Vermont in June; he would be commissioned in the Army and depart for his first assignment not long thereafter.

In the community, neighbors could not believe we would trade Vermont for Arkansas, but having visited the previous September, Ann would simply ask them if they had ever been there and point out all of its advantages, such as the vibrant communities, outdoor recreation, and scenic beauty of northern Arkansas. I let the Boy Scouts know I was leaving, and as an experiment I showed the seven boys I was counseling for their Citizenship in the Nation Merit Badge a blank map of the United States and asked them to point out Arkansas. Six of the seven were not even close. The one who was able to identify it was the one who was home schooled and had actually studied geography; my wife had been urging the school board to restore geography to the curriculum for the past ten years only to have the "educators" assure her that it was covered within other courses. She was quick to point this out to the superintendent as a reminder of why she kept suggesting that geography be included in the curriculum. Too many school systems today fail to teach the geography of our country, as well as civics to ensure the graduates actually understand how our government works.

After all the places we have lived, we love Little Rock and find it to be a terrific small city. It has been described as a twenty-minute town, in that you can get almost anywhere you want in twenty minutes or less. There are wonderful restaurants throughout the city, the Arkansas Symphony Orchestra is superb, the Little Rock Zoo is a nice place for grandchildren to visit, and there are tremendous medical services with three tertiary care hospitals for adults, a renowned children's hospital, and the Veterans Administration Medical Center along the Interstate 630 corridor.

We bought a home in the LaMarche subdivision on the same street as my friend Joe Smith from the NCPE. The airport is convenient, and it is hard to imagine an easier place for all of our family to be able to visit. One of my first personnel actions was to convince Dr. Connie Meeks to move to Little Rock to fill a new position as Corporate Medical Director for Internal Affairs, focused on actions within ABCBS. She was replaced as Medical Director for Northeast Arkansas by Dr. Bert Price from Jonesboro, bringing additional talent to ABCBS. I knew from our time in the Army that he was strong both in psychiatry and in clinical medicine, and his leadership always had brought out the best in those with whom he worked. The next personnel move was equally important: creating a Corporate Medical Director for External Affairs and hiring Victor (Vic) Snyder, MD, as he retired from the U.S. Congress. He had a tremendous reputation as a family practice physician and the personality and talent to establish closer ties to the primary care practices as we worked hard to decrease their administrative burden. With my retirement, Dr. Meeks was offered and assumed my position, and the same with Dr. Price regarding hers, confirming my philosophy of finding and bringing in talented professionals and then further developing them for success.

I am extremely proud of my time with ABCBS and like to think that my service in Arkansas helped repay this great state for the warm welcome my family received back in 1959. There were several accomplishments, but the one that I believed helped the most Arkansans was guiding Niki Wilson, RN, Director of Enterprise Medical Management, with the design and implementation of a medical management program that had registered nurses serving as case managers in every county across the state to support the Exchange population under the Private Option. These nurses would perform a comprehensive assessment of ABCBS members to determine their greatest needs; their medical, behavioral, financial, and social services status; and their knowledge regarding behaviors impacting health. They would then link them up with Arkansas state resources and their community agencies. These case managers would meet with our members in a community setting or in their homes, prepare them for doctor visits, and accompany them if needed. They would then follow up with them to make sure that they understood their condition and had the ability to comply with their physicians' instructions.

We also executed a centralized care management program on a national basis under the leadership of Sandra New, RN, DNP, Director of National Account Medical Management, and Dr. Joanna Thomas, MD, Corporate Medical Director for National Accounts, reaching out to members across the country to provide similar services telephonically.

Most important to me from the time of my return to Arkansas to my retirement from ABCBS was knowing that I had built upon Dr. Jim Adamson's solid foundation and legacy to add a first-class care management program to his nationally recognized program for primary coverage criteria. This program had a national reputation as the most academically rigorous program for this across the country. I know that nothing lasts forever, so I consider my legacy to be the talent that I brought to the company, and I feel very comfortable that those who followed me will continue to develop those who follow them.

Letterman Army Medical Center, Presidio of San Francisco, where Griffin was a pediatric intern from 1974 to 1975 and a general surgery resident from 1977 to 1981. On the top five floors at the end of the hospital toward the bay, each ward had a sunroom projecting off each floor. These solariums were primarily for the inpatients during the day, but the medical and surgical residents and staff would frequently gather in one of the tenth-floor solariums early in the morning to watch the sunrise to the east and then watch to the west as the sun illuminated the Golden Gate Bridge.

View of Alcatraz Island from Letterman Army Medical Center. Buildings in the foreground are part of the Presidio.

Expert Field Medical Badge (EFMB) training in Panama led by Major Robert Griffin; 1975.

Field medical training at Fort Ord, California, assembling a Medical Unit Self Transportable (MUST) as part of field medical training; 1979. In 1980, Griffin would deploy to Europe with the 47th Combat Support Hospital for a Return of Forces to Germany (REFORGER) Exercise, where he would be performing surgery in this type of facility.

Griffin as a senior surgical resident at Letterman Army Medical Center with the emergency entrance in background; 1980.

July RFG on temporary duty as a general surgeon at 47th CSH in Germany for REFORGER exercise in northern part of West Germany; 1980.

Griffin in Bad Kreuznach as 8th Infantry Division Surgeon with LTC Jim Wortham, Commander of 8th Medical Battalion on REFORGER exercise; 1983.

Griffin (center) in Bad Kreuznach as 8th Infantry Division Surgeon visiting a MUST hospital with his medical section staff during a REFORGER exercise; 1983. CPT Price is on LTC Griffin's left and then CPT Wilkinson on far left. Hospital MUST ward is in the rear.

8th Infantry Division Command and Staff, MG Dyke is on the front row, fourth from left, LTC Dave Arthur is on the second row right, and Griffin is in the back row, second from left; spring 1984. (U.S. Army Photo)

MG Charles W. Dyke holding Carolyn (today an Air Force Major) after presenting a Meritorious Service Medal to Robert Griffin, with Ann.

Griffin, commanding the Third Medical Battalion (3d MED BN) in Germany during RE-FORGER exercises conducting a situation briefing near Adelsried, West Germany; September 1984.

UH1 medical helicopter on station for REFORGER; September 1974.

Family gathering in a field setting after REFORGER exercise; October 1974.

Staff spouses in the field after REFORGER. (Left to right) Debbie Brinker, Carol Agee, Ann Griffin, and Barbara Kindred.

In 1985, 3d MED BN *received fifteen tracked ambulances. Exercises were conducted to train in using these ambulances from the front lines to a transfer point where casualties would be transferred to wheeled ambulances for faster evacuation farther to the rear.*

LTC Griffin and LTC Nekola, Commander of the German 12th Medical Battalion and 3d MED BN Partnership unit, visiting together in the field; April 1985.

COL Paul Vanderploog seated at the Officers' Club with his DISCOM battalion commanders, left to right: LTCs Beauchamp, Culwell, Griffin, Champion, Hoose, and Andrews; 1985.

COL Griffin (center) with staff from left to right: MAJ Kindred, CPT Giddens, CPT Trent, and CPT Inouye at a military ceremony.

Colonel Vanderploog and Ann Griffin at the promotion of Robert Griffin to Colonel; April 1, 1985.

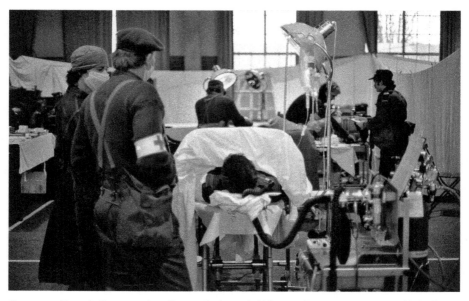

Operation Danish Bacon with a Denmark Army field hospital operating room established in a village school outside Copenhagen where Colonel Griffin was an observer; 1985.

128th Combat Support Hospital operating in a German Army fixed hospital facility in Bamberg, West Germany; 1986. Left to right: Abs. Sara Kostler, German Chief Nurse; MAJ Rosemary Robinson, Unit Chief Nurse; LTC Meg Cline, Exercise Chief Nurse, with COL Griffin, Exercise Commander.

REFORGER Exercise, 128th Combat Support Hospital Ambulance Train at station 1; 1986.

REFORGER Exercise, 128th Combat Support Hospital Ambulance Train at station 2; 1986.

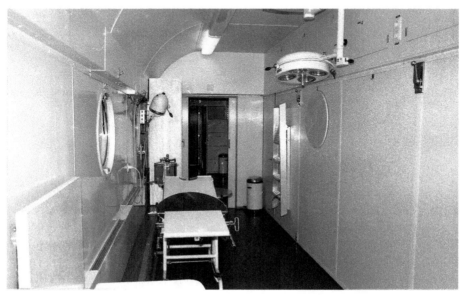

REFORGER Exercise, 128th Combat Support Hospital Ambulance Train Operating Room Car; 1986.

REFORGER Exercise, 128th Combat Support Hospital Ambulance Train Ward Car; 1986.

MG Ledford, CG 7th MEDCOM presiding over transfer of command from Colonel Robert Claypool to Colonel Robert Griffin by presenting unit colors to Griffin; July 15, 1987.

Robert and Ann prepare to depart to a formal event with German Partners in 1988.

Ann and Robert at a formal military dinner in 1988.

Laura Griffin (in pink dress on left) and Carolyn Griffin (in light blue dress on right) participate as flower girls for a wedding of German friends.

Soldiers of 2d Armored Cavalry Regiment (ACR) prepare for inspection prior to border patrol where COL Sutton, Ann Griffin, and Robert Griffin will accompany them to the actual border.

West Point classmates and physicians Colonels Reggie Moore (left) and Robert Griffin meet in Riyadh for Thanksgiving dinner during Operation Desert Shield.

Surprise reunion in the desert between CSM Lawrence Williams and COL Griffin, who had been the leadership team at the 98th General Hospital.

Gulf War arrival of tracked ambulance at port; January 1991.

332 Medical Brigade Leaders (left to right) COL Fulfer, BG Strong, COL Griffin, and COL Smith in the desert.

332 Medical Brigade Command and Staff. Front row, from left: COL Paul Holland, COL Robert Griffin, COL Bob Smith, BG Mike Strong, COL Reggie Moore, COL Dalton Diamond, and COL Jesse Fulfer. (U.S. Army Photo)

COL Griffin in desert visiting forward medical team during Gulf War.

Evacuation Hospital ready for casualties in Saudi Arabia; February 1991.

COL Griffin and BG Strong (left) link up in Iraq to exchange information regarding medical unit and logistical status during Desert Storm.

COL Griffin with LTG Fred Franks in Iraq during Desert Storm.

Tom Griffin at home in Germany guarding the front door in Robert's absence.

Keller Army Community Hospital West Point, where Griffin was the 45th USMA Surgeon and the Commander of the hospital and Medical Department Activities.

West Point football hospital tailgate party; 1992. Chaplain (Colonel) Calvin Sydnor (center) from VII Corps came to visit.

West Point football hospital tailgate party; 1992. Tom is on the Army Mule.

Laura, Carolyn, and Tom in Fayetteville, Georgia, in 1994.

Fluffy the bunny, who demonstrated the advantage of positive stimuli over negative.

Tom, Laura, and Carolyn in Fayetteville, Georgia, in 1994.

Robert Griffin promoted to Brigadier General at Fort McPherson, Georgia, by GEN Tilelli with Ann's assistance; December 1995.

In 1996, Griffin was assigned as Deputy Commanding General of the U.S. Army Medical Command, Chief of Medical Corps Career Activities, and Head of the Army Medical Contracting Activity at Fort Sam Houston, Texas, and the family was assigned Quarters 10, the Jim Bowie House.

Tom, Ann, Laura, and Carolyn on the front porch of Quarters 10; April 1997.

Fort Gordon, Georgia, on the first day at Episcopal Day School in Augusta. Carolyn, Laura, and Tom stand in front of Quarters 4, a converted hunting cabin on Boardman Lake.

Never realizing we would later move to Little Rock, Arkansas, Tom chose Arkansas for his school project in which he had to select a state to research and make a presentation on for the class.

Acceptance ceremony for the first Army C-12 Medical Transport Aircraft for the Southeast Regional Medical Command.

Griffin formally retires from the Army in 1999 at Fort Gordon, Georgia, and receives the casing from his final cannon salute from CSM Wang with LTG Blanck.

Robert and Ann Griffin at their farewell dinner at Fort Gordon, Georgia.

Fort Gordon RFG retirement, last military move; 1999.

University of Arkansas, Peabody Hall, formerly University High School in Fayetteville, Arkansas, at the time of the RFG fifty-year reunion; 2012.

Section 3: Observations and Thoughts on Leadership

Prior to World War II, promotion in the Army was stagnant and officers and noncommissioned officers would remain in grade for many years waiting for a vacancy to advance. During World War II, the Army had to expand rapidly. There was little time for leader development, so the process was rushed. My father advanced from lieutenant to lieutenant colonel in less than three years. Following the war, several officers were reduced in rank commensurate with their seniority and experience. Going forward, it was recognized that this was not a sustainable model for the future and promotion "gates" were established for officers to either be selected for promotion or be released from active duty. There was an active design in the Army to develop leaders so there would be a greater nucleus of experienced leaders for a potential rapid expansion in the future. The same was true of enlisted soldiers and noncommissioned officers. The old Technical or Specialist ranks which allowed for promotion without leadership requirements have been eliminated above the junior enlisted ranks, and there are similar gates beyond which an officer cannot remain if he or she is not selected for promotion. The term for this is "up or out."

Civilian organizations generally do not require leadership for retention. There are numerous fields in which employees may serve at an entry level as long as they are productive, even an entire career. Generally there is a salary band for levels, above which pure retention no longer produces a salary increase, but productivity and incentive bonuses exist to promote retention of top performers who either choose not to become leaders or know they lack the skills required for leadership. Becoming a leader is an option, but there are both rewards and risks. Once a person moves into the leadership sphere, it is difficult to go back within the same unit or organization, so he or she must lead well or move on.

The first line of leadership in most organizations is the supervisor, though some may recognize a team leader position below that. Generally you must apply for the position and you will be selected based upon your potential more than your past performance in a previous or current position, though performance history is a major consideration in the selection process. Other considerations may include education, experience, specialized training, and a positive interview. The most important consideration, though, is your perceived potential in a leadership role. Only a foolish senior leader would select a direct reporting leader based upon friendship or as a reward for a single event, as failure of a lower-level leader can cause failure of leaders one or even two levels higher.

Before applying for a leadership position, one should examine his or her motives in doing so. The best motive is the desire to make a real difference in the organization and improve morale and productivity among those to be led. The worst is a simple desire for more money, perceived power or authority, or prestige—any one of which could ultimately progress to embarrassment, failure, and termination.

Leadership is generally a learned skill. Natural-born leaders exist, but they are rare. For the rest of us, it requires study, observation, practice, honest self-reflection, and self-discipline to be effective leaders. I am not a natural leader, and for me this was a hard and sometimes painful effort.

In general, within organizations, there are two types of leaders: thought leaders and leaders of people. Occasionally, an individual may fill both functions, but for the most part it is difficult to accomplish both simultaneously. Each requires a certain background, education level, experience level, imagination, and level of expertise. Both leadership roles require a substantial time commitment to be effective, which often is problematic, particularly for the thought leaders, for whom this is often a secondary role.

Unfortunately, thought leaders rarely have a designated position within organizations such as chief of strategy or plans. More commonly, they are not formally recognized but spend their spare time thinking about how things could be done quicker, easier, and/or better. They tend to self-select, and their peers and astute leaders of people know who they are and turn to them with problems to solve. They have the ability not only to develop new products or processes, but they also are able to communicate these ideas effectively. It is important that organizations formally recognize these individuals and reward them appropriately for their achievements. An astute leader of people will know exactly how to do this on an individualized basis. If this is not a full-time position, recognition of the contribution can be accomplished with public recognition programs, additional time off with pay, and special incentive payments. Although this text is dedicated to the development of leaders of people, the value of the thought leaders and their contributions must be recognized.

Leaders of people undergo a different selection process. They are selected to fill specific designated leadership positions in the organization. In general, there are defined prerequisites such as education, experience, and/or training, and there should be a formal recruitment or selection process that guarantees an equal opportunity for those that meet the prerequisites to be considered and selected. This process generally identifies the best candidate and leads to the greatest probability of success. Internal candidates are generally identified through documented performance, while external candidates are identified through a recruitment process which generally calls for some specific formal education and experience in similar settings. No matter which basis is used for identification, the selection really comes down to perceived potential to inspire, coach, counsel, mentor, and develop others. This is not the time to "take care of a friend," as failure will inevitably occur and unfavorably impact the individual, the individual's next higher leader, and the organization.

As noted, promotion of leaders of people is based to a very high extent upon the collective performance over time of those individuals who have been led. The first step in becoming a leader is all about you. Significant emphasis will be focused on what you have accomplished, how well you have prepared yourself, and what others have thought or said about your potential. However, future steps on the leadership path are all about those whom you led—how well they have performed under your leadership and what they accomplished on your behalf. Pick the wrong leaders to report to you, and you may find yourself at a dead end in the organization and seeking new employment if these leaders have not produced to expectations and you have been unwilling or unable to fix responsibility, hold these leaders accountable, and insist upon better results.

Going forward as a new leader, you must realize that it is all about "the team," not "your team." Previously, you were likely one of the functional experts, but as a full-time leader your direct performing skills will decay. Any light that shines on a leader should be reflected to the one or ones that did the work and earned the credit. The more this happens, the better the team will perform and the more light there will be to reflect. If ideas and accomplishments of individual team members do not reflect on those doing the work, there will be fewer new ideas and fewer accomplishments beyond the baseline level. You, as the leader, must have real pride in their accomplishments, mention them often in multiple settings, and make sure that your leader is aware and even comments on specific accomplishments directly to the individual worker and junior leaders responsible. Bringing a senior leader in the organization to a single operational unit to thank a specific person for a single significant success will produce enormous dividends.

The military and the corporate world are similar in the roles and responsibilities as people rise in the chain of command or organizational structure. There are tactical, day-to-day production-based roles which flow upward from the individual worker and include performance of specific duties, identification of innovation to improve quality and production, upward communication of good ideas, and a focus on safety. These roles all fall under the purview of a manager or equivalent leadership position.

Strategic roles flow down from the board of directors, president or chief executive officer, and executive staff. They include the development and communication of a mission, a vision, a strategy, values, cultures, and behaviors, and the allocation of mission-essential resources. In a great organization safety is paramount. Recall the words of MG Dyke, who said that in the Army, nothing done in peacetime warrants the loss of life or limb. With the exception of emergency first responders, this is even more true in the civilian world. With these words the 8th Infantry Division immediately adopted a culture of safety in training.

Finally, if you choose to be a leader, to be successful you must have and maintain the moral authority to lead people. It is important to set and maintain boundaries. If a leader regularly socializes with one or two team members, to the exclusion of the others, this will sow jealousy and discontent, and eventually the results will be harvested, to the leader's and the institution's detriment. Leading former peers is hard, but leading friends is even harder. Fair or not, people judge others by how they behave, both in private and in public, and some people will exploit these vulnerabilities if they see them. The higher a person is in the organization, the more visible they become, and their behavior both on the job and in the community will often drive similar behavior. If leaders cut corners, are lax with the truth, take unfair advantage of others, misappropriate funds or steal from the organization, or cheat on their spouse, partners, or the organization, others will feel empowered to behave in a similar fashion and the organization will either purge these people or this will become the corporate culture by default.

It is crucial to understand that each level in an organization requires a different skill set. Sometimes this is a modification of skills that created success at the prior level and easily pass to the next. However, overall, the skills for success vary from level to level and a rising leader must adapt with the transition from one level to another. In short, the levels are as follows:

- President/Chief Executive Officer: Leader of Leaders of Leaders of Leaders of Leaders of Leaders who Lead Workers
- Chief Operating Officer: Leader of Leaders of Leaders of Leaders of Leaders who Lead Workers
- Vice President: Leader of Leaders of Leaders of Leaders who Lead Workers
- Director: Leader of Leaders of Leaders who Lead Workers
- Manager: Leader of Leaders who Lead Workers
- Supervisor: Leader of Workers
- Worker: One who does the work

There is a great difference between what the individual worker sees and does every day versus what the chief executive officer may see on a daily basis, having instead to rely upon records and reports from a succession of different leaders (or perhaps filters) between that person and the individual worker. This brings to mind an observation I noted previously as a young lieutenant in Vietnam regarding the 5,000-foot view of our battalion commander seeing "footprints in the sand." In general, I have concluded that depending on the size, mission, and scope of an organization, the directors or vice presidents have a 5,000-foot view of what is happening in the organization while the president, chief executive officer, and the Board of Directors may have anywhere between the 40,000-foot view from a commercial airliner to the International Space Station view.

As I advanced through successive leadership levels, this image haunted me. I came to the realization that in order for me to have direct visibility of what a single soldier or worker would be doing on any given day, the time spent doing so would be limiting my field of vision to anywhere from 1 of 50 to 1 of 7,500 of the individuals within my leadership responsibilities. Clearly, I had to learn to accept that loss of granularity and trust that I had the right leaders in the right positions for their skills, that I had ensured that they had the necessary education and training for their position, and that I had given them the right guidance and set the right environment for them to be successful. Furthermore, it was incumbent upon me to make sure that my communications to the people working were accurate, without any "spin," and that the information I received in return was not being filtered so that I would only see the good news. The key, therefore, was to verify with the occasional, relatively quick "spot checks." (Also known as "Trust but Verify.")

A great portion of my success came because I had learned how to lead or manage without being either too close to or too distant from the critical production points. This leads to the following key points for leaders:

- The perspective changes with height.
- The higher you are, the more you see, but the less detail you are able to see.
- As a leader of leaders, you are likely no longer the real subject matter expert and you do not always appreciate the real or potential distractions.
- A senior leader's role is more and more focused on mission and direction, not execution, but senior leaders are accountable for execution.
- If seniors pick the person and give specific instructions, they likely will not get the same quality of results as if they selected the leader, communicated what was needed and why, and allowed the leader to plan and execute (keeping the leader and senior leader informed, as needed).
- A senior leader cannot (and should not try to) know everything—neither can those who directly report to the senior leader, but all of the leaders in the chain should conduct "spot checks" and have workers explain what they are doing and ask how it could be done better.
- Learn to accept, better yet, encourage, the use of briefers (experts that are directly involved in activity) for in-progress reports
  - Gives the briefer and intermediate leaders exposure to higher leaders
  - Grants the senior leader the opportunity to publicly thank them for great work
- Bypassing intermediate leaders and "taking charge" undercuts the

leaders bypassed.

Another key concept that must be understood is that of "institutional energy." Think of this like a cell phone. The phone has a maximum charge which reflects the energy available. The more calls made, apps used, texts sent, photos taken, or internet sites surfed, the more energy used. The battery drains, and less charge, if any, will be left at the end of the day. At least daily, and occasionally more frequently, you must recharge the battery.

Every organization has a potential level of institutional energy. This is not a finite number, and it is difficult if not impossible to calculate. It comes from the staffing numbers and their level of skills, education, and training. The energy is consumed based upon the efficiency of the staff, the nature and complexity of tasks, efficiency of operations, and the ease of use of the facility. It is incumbent upon leaders to understand this concept, use the institutional energy wisely, and avoid diversion of the energy to a non-productive activity. Unfortunately, because a key component of institutional energy consists of the efforts of real people, while there are a number of ways to drain this institutional energy there are very few ways to recharge it. Examples of nonproductive drains of institutional energy by leaders include the following:

- Artificially or unnecessarily heightening the sense of anxiety
- Using hyperbole to make a point
- Overreacting to problems and issues
- "Shooting the messengers" when they bring you news you need to hear but don't want to hear
- Musing about ideas in front of direct reports without letting them know that you are thinking out loud and do not want a "white paper" on the subject
- Setting or accepting unrealistic expectations and insisting that the organization do more with less until you expect them to do everything with nothing
- Promoting initiatives without resources, creating a resource-requirement mismatch

Most working Americans have a substantial degree of loyalty to their organization and are committed to see it thrive. They understand what is important and will make great efforts to meet expectations. On the other hand, hyperbole can and will eventually make them numb. A great example of this was when I was a young lieutenant training for Vietnam. As a motivator, almost everything we were being taught began with "You have to learn this particular skill well or you will be killed in Vietnam." For a very short period, this heightened our attention, but soon the indiscriminate use of this phrase caused us all to begin thinking there were so many ways to get killed that we were going to die there whether we learned a particular lesson or not. Consequently, instead of paying close attention, we tuned out the offending instructor when we should not have. This same effect can happen in corporate America when more senior leaders consistently overstate the criticality of a particular initiative, program, activity, or customer. Instead of overstating everything, use the heightened urgency selectively and save the mission-critical rhetoric for mission-critical situations. You will get a magnificent response. Overuse this type of intensity and you will generate mediocrity.

As to verbalizing your musings, I learned this lesson late in my career and the hard way. When I took my first command as a general officer, it wasn't too long before I made the mistake of doing just that. I don't even remember the subject, as it was quite minor, but I do remember that two weeks after chatting with my two deputies and just sharing my thoughts about an idea, I was presented with a 500-plus-page white paper exploring the pros and cons of the issue. This was much to my embarrassment, as it represented really great but truly unnecessary work by several people. Thereafter, I was careful to either keep my thoughts to myself until I was actually considering the need for action or make sure that everyone knew that I only wanted to "bounce" some ideas off of them but did not want an elaborate study performed.

It is incumbent upon leaders to define and review their required tasks, the conditions under which tasks must be met, and the standards to which they must adhere. These things must be analyzed on a regular basis and adjusted accordingly. I am a strong proponent of zero-based budgeting rather than receiving an incremental budget based upon the prior year(s), whether used efficiently or not. In a zero-based budget, requirements are defined in advance and resources are requested or designated based upon the tasks, conditions, and standards to meet the requirement. If resources available or obtainable are insufficient, then the requirements must be adjusted or the tasks, conditions, and standards must be altered to match the available resources.

This balancing can be done by adjusting the tasks involved, conditions under which the tasks must be performed, or the performance standards. For example, in the insurance industry, if the standard for the turnaround time for processing a paper claim is one business day, this may need to be adjusted to two business days, requiring fewer resources. Balancing this is hard work and hard decisions must be made. An imbalance may work in the short run, but in the long run, having too many resources yields inefficiency and waste while having too few resources leads to frustration. A note on terminology: If you are learning leadership from academic presentations (which this is not intended to be), you will often be told that the primary tools of leadership are **power, authority**, and **influence**. If you search under these terms, you will find them referred to frequently and with similar, but slightly different, definitions and contextual settings. At any given time, a leader may want to draw upon these tools which may be, at least in theory, available to him or her. It is possible to have power with no authority and authority without power. For the purpose of this discussion, I will provide the definitions that I use for these terms.

Power is the ability to force someone to take a certain action or inaction. In theory, this force may be physical or it may involve other punitive measures, but there is an implicit threat in the use of power. It is coercive in nature and unilateral in application. In reality, the only tools of power are guns, knives, blunt instruments such as baseball bats, and incarceration. Any use of these tools would be an assault, and any threat to do so would be on the wrong side of multiple laws and regulations. A popular example of perceived power would be a military leader who relied on the Uniform Code of Military Justice with the ability to criminalize disobedience instead of applying positive leadership. However, even this would require multiple levels of review, investigations, and a court-martial (military trial) to carry out. The truth is that power in leadership is really an illusion.

Authority is the institutional right to limit behavior to certain desired choices. It is formal and belongs to the institution and is generally subject to labor laws. That is to say, you can limit choices, but in general, the subject of the limitation may refuse and leave the institution without harm to the individual but perhaps with harm to the organization by failure to execute and the need to hire and train a replacement. It is also coercive, but it is bilateral, in that the subject does have a choice to comply or resign. Authority generally can be delegated, but the responsibility that goes with it cannot. An example might be the decision for suspension without pay for a violation of company policy being limited to the vice-presidential level and subject to internal review.

Influence is the ability to cause others to voluntarily choose the alternative favored by the influencer. It is generally informal, persuasive rather than coercive, and bilateral. It quickly became my tool of choice. An example could be convincing an employee to pay extra attention to a specific action by explaining the importance and potential impact of the action.

Frankly, after graduating from West Point, I began my career enamored with power and authority until I realized that these characteristics were more commonly seen in use by those I considered to be poor leaders. I had to correct this character flaw or I would become a poor leader as well. These leaders did not draw upon the intelligence and strengths of the soldiers involved, and they were more likely to get satisfactory but not optimal results. While I maintained the possible use of power (through military law) and authority in my leadership toolbox during my military career and I also had substantial authority in my corporate positions, I rarely used these tools. When I had to do so, I felt that either I was compelled to do so by time and urgency requirements or that I had failed as a leader.

To the extent possible, I prefer a participatory style of leadership. Whenever I can, I use or encourage the use of three phases for decision making and implementation. The first phase is a discussion phase. I like to entertain all viewpoints, specifically those that go against my first impression. I often start the discussion phase with the lowest-rated member of the team and move upward in the discussion. This way all have the opportunity to speak without being impressed with or biased by the experience of those who may actually no longer be the real subject matter experts. Next is the decision phase. This may belong to a single, accountable leader, or it may be delegated to a small decision-making group. This is often driven by time available and the criticality of the mission. The higher the criticality and urgency, such as in armed combat, the less time there is available for discussion. This is the call of the leader who ultimately bears the responsibility for both the timeliness and the efficacy of the decision.

In a new leadership role, you need to play the hand that you were dealt. The team members are not "your team," but, in today's society, they are your fellow citizens who share the same work space and rely on you for direction and leadership. Employees are frequently one of the greatest expenses and assets for a corporation. They must be recruited, accessed into the organization, oriented, trained, and given the opportunity to succeed. Constantly replacing trained employees who leave the organization due to the practices of a poor leader is prohibitively expensive for the organization, and before long, that leader will be terminated. A leader's primary role is to give direction, educate, coach, mentor, counsel, instill a sense of discipline, and hold poor performers accountable for their results. Where leaders identify strengths, they should reinforce them. Where leaders identify weaknesses, they should provide additional training and coaching to overcome them. As a last resort, when after remedial education, training opportunities, and counseling, the skills cannot be acquired or properly applied to accomplish the required tasks to the defined standards, leaders may need to terminate an employee. However, before doing so, the organization must make sure that the best efforts to improve the performance of the individual were made and that the leaders properly documented shortcomings including the guidance and the training that was provided, the development of a correction plan, and the opportunity to execute that program. Also make absolutely sure that the leaders have followed the rules of the organization and have complied with the requisite state and federal laws pertaining to personnel management. There are no shortcuts. Remember, if an organization attempts to take disciplinary action against an employee and loses because a leader skipped a step or two, it will be substantially harder to take action against that employee at a later date for the same or similar behavior. However, I have found that evil doers will do evil again and if documentation is not sufficient and the organization does not act precipitously, the individual will oblige you by providing additional factors to document until you have a defendable case.

There are many traits that I have observed over the years that cause leaders to fail by losing the confidence of their employees and ultimately their employer. In many ways it is more important to understand this than it is to understand how to succeed, as you can fail quickly and spectacularly, but it often takes time for your leaders to judge that you will not be successful and you may have time to adapt. Following is a list of some of these traits that can lead to failure:

Damaging Personal Traits
- Being unapproachable
- Being inconsistent
- Interrupting and not listening
- Nitpicking
- Bullying
- Being indecisive

Leadership Deficiencies
- Adopting a rigid approach to everything
- Never explaining why
- Displaying a condescending attitude toward team member(s)
- Demonstrating ingratitude—rarely praising and thanking
- Having a tendency to watch the lane of others rather than your own
- Yielding to the unofficial influencers that can poison an organization

Toxic Leadership Styles
- Managing by intimidation
- Invading personal space to make a point
- Taking all of the credit
- Failing to assume responsibility
- Asking someone to do the impossible so you can wash your hands of it and shift blame
- Sharing blame with the team rather than taking responsibility as the leader
- Focusing all of the blame on the team if things don't go well
- Playing favorites
- Micromanaging by always handling or involving yourself in minor details when staff members are fully capable without your help

Fatal Personal Characteristics
- Demonstrating unethical behavior
- Lying, cheating, and stealing

- Creating, allowing, or fostering perceptions of impropriety
- Harassing people

Let's break this down a little further. The list is divided into four categories. Each category will be addressed separately, but it is important to emphasize that as a leader, you will have a relationship with each of your direct reports and, if they are also leaders, a secondary relationship to each of theirs. This relationship will primarily be driven by you and will not be the same with each individual, but it must be equivalent to all at each level. Keeping in mind that your success depends virtually 100% on their success, you must drive that relationship. Further, it is far easier to establish a great working relationship up front than to repair a damaged relationship, particularly when the damage was due to your actions or guidance. You must assess the needs of each individual, contemplate how you wish to approach them, and work to establish a relationship of mutual trust and respect. All of these points directly impact the person you are going to lead, but other people whom you lead will observe how you treat their peers and this will influence them as well. They will not trust you if you do not trust them, and they will not respect you if you do not respect each of them. All of the points above are harmful to human relations, and if you treat one person in this regard, the others will feel in jeopardy that you will treat them the same way at some point. You cannot indulge in these behaviors, but if you inadvertently do so, once you reflect on how you reacted, you should apologize promptly and with meaning. Remember, you are as human as those you lead.

The damaging personal traits identified will not, in and of themselves, preclude success, but they will make it significantly more difficult for your team to accomplish its goals and results will be reliant not upon your leadership capability, but upon their degree of professionalism. In the absence of guidance, some will establish their own guidance, others will rely on their peers, and others will simply flounder. All will avoid returning to you for clarification, and the results likely will not be what you were actually looking for. Misunderstandings will emerge and multiply.

The leadership deficiencies also may take some time to derail you. The issue regarding watching your own lane rather than that of others is a far too common practice in business. The terminology is in reference to "Lane Training," a significant part of infantry training. During this training, a squad (eight to ten soldiers) will advance on foot toward an objective; the soldiers are placed in a line, far enough apart so they can see the next person over, and move along a designated course toward the objective. Along the way they will encounter prepositioned aggressor forces potentially mixed in with non-combatants. Each lane will have an evaluator following the soldier. The intent is to make sure that each soldier clears his or her own lane, accounting for quick decision making regarding whether an individual encountered is hostile, as rapid decisive action must be taken against the hostile actor but not the non-combatant. Failure to watch your lane in combat may be fatal. In the civilian world, if you are busy watching someone else's lane instead of your own, you will not accomplish your own mission well. For example, if a manager is too busy watching over a supervisor in someone else's department, the work in this manager's department will suffer, and the manager should, and likely will, be held accountable. Likewise, an employee worrying too much about how much easier someone else appears to have it likely will be unaware of other requirements upon the employee observed and will be held accountable for the work that he or she did not do while watching the other person.

The toxic leadership styles will likely lead to poor results and substantial personnel management problems. This will stimulate adverse behavior in your team. Some will mimic your approach in dealing with others, while some will adopt a passive-aggressive approach in which they will give minimal effort and deliberately misconstrue the guidance they are given rather than returning to you for clarification. Some will even allow errors to occur so long as they can avoid assuming any more blame than would be attributed to them anyway, and particularly if they can shift the blame back to you. Others will be frequently meeting with the Human Resources staff and will lodge multiple complaints and eventually transfer within the organization or resign, creating the significant financial and time burdens of recruiting, interviewing, hiring, and training replacements. All will fail to give you their best effort.

The fatal personal characteristics will inevitably come out and you will have no defense.

Success is a long-term project. In order to succeed, everyone must know and understand the definition of success for their specific role—a fact that should be obvious but often is not. A leader must have a clear comprehension of their organization's mission, culture, and values. Everyone must know their team's specific role and how that interacts with and impacts the other parts of the organization. Using a term from chemistry, leaders need to determine the "rate limiting" part of the equation in terms of both input to the team and its anticipated output, and how that fits in the broader perspective. A leader's intent must be clear to all.

From there, return to the tasks, conditions, and standards previously discussed when one first assumes a leadership role and periodically thereafter. My preference was to do a limited review at the onset of the annual budget cycle and a comprehensive review every two years even if the budget was not zero based, but this will not fit every situation. Doing this allows a leader to determine or confirm the requirements for the team so that the leader can allocate resources and establish priorities in a logical and defendable manner. This may identify requirements for additional technology, education, and training both for continuous operations and for unique unanticipated surges in requirements. A leader's responsibility is to make sure that this all comes together in a manner that produces excellent, timely results to support the organizational mission.

It is important to set and communicate clear expectations as to what leaders expect from those they lead and what they can expect from the leader in return. I strongly recommend publishing a philosophy memorandum or letter, and I have placed a sample from one of my past positions at the end of this book (Appendix 2). I've also included my vision statement for the Southeast Army Regional Medical Command, July 1997, as Appendix 1. In developing your individual philosophy statement, give careful thought to what you say, as you will have to hold yourself responsible for adhering to it; if you fail to do so, you will lose credibility and someone will eventually point this out to you at the most awkward time. This memorandum will give those you lead a basis to understand what is important to you and will serve as a general compass for them. It also empowers them against the unofficial influencers, as they cannot "spin" what you have put in writing as opposed to verbally communicated where words may take on different meanings. Be consistent in what you say, what you do, and how you treat others. Do not allow perceptions of favoritism to develop. Remind all that loyalty is bidirectional and that you expect loyalty from the people on your team, and in return you will be loyal to them. However, remind them that all have a duty to be loyal to the institution, and that trumps loyalty to individuals in both directions as well.

Another tool that I have found to be particularly useful is to schedule a biweekly one-on-one meeting with each of my direct reports. Since I can approach them anytime that I need to do so, I defer the agenda for these meetings to them. They are not mandatory, so if they do not need or wish to discuss an issue of concern, seek guidance, or simply engage in a general discussion, they may cancel without penalty. On the other hand, I make every effort to keep these appointments, and if I really cannot meet at the scheduled time, I make sure that I find an alternate time that will be convenient for the individual. I may use these sessions to lavish particular praise for a job well done, but I never use these sessions for criticism or admonition. I schedule these sessions separately.

This leads into the need for and importance of counseling. In the Army, noncommissioned officers (sergeants) are the front-line leaders who get things done. Collectively, they emphasize what they refer to as "footlocker counseling," which refers to routine counseling sessions with a fairly typical format. These sessions invariably start with what is going right and what the soldier is doing well (there is always something). This is followed by identifying together what the soldier could potentially do better and discussing what this would take. This is where they talk about selected military readings, additional training programs, extra physical fitness time, and skills development training or education. Together a plan is made to initiate this, and it is the responsibility of the leader to allocate the time and resources discussed to the soldier and the soldier sets the time frame to conduct the training and evaluate progress. This works equally well at the first-line supervisor level in most industries. Keep in mind that one of the key roles of leaders as they move up in organizations is to identify and develop those emerging leaders that will ultimately move up in turn. These sessions will help accomplish this. All too often, I have heard the complaint that identifying and developing emerging leaders is an incredible effort, and indeed it is. It must be so, given the future ramifications of having the best-prepared leaders moving up in the organization. As noted previously, the higher a leader moves up in an organization the more he or she must trust the capabilities of those in line behind. One of the worst failures of a senior leader is to not develop the next cohort to take his or her place; this effort precludes that from occurring.

When I commanded the 3d Medical Battalion, I reported to the commander of the Division Support Command, Colonel Paul Vanderploog. I learned as much or more from him than from any other single leader I encountered. Much of the guidance found in this document is derived from his wisdom. From the onset, he insisted that any information brought to him must either be verifiable (100% accurate) or qualified (the degree of confidence) and complete. He was fine with yes, no, or I'll find out answers, as well as answers such as "I am about x% sure, but will confirm and get back to you" (assuming that this was not a detail that the person really should have known). In the Army, where life-and-death decisions must be made, the degree of accuracy is essential for contingency planning purposes.

Another important lesson of a similar nature came from Major General Dyke, who let all of us on his staff know in no uncertain terms that we must never, ever preempt his decision-making capability by not bringing something to his attention that he needed to know. In retrospect, I realized that I had recognized the concept, but not put it into words, during my medical school years. I noticed that some of the brighter-appearing young physicians in training (medical students, interns, and residents) would often come to a conclusion regarding an individual patient and when presenting the case to the attending physician, they tended to provide only the information that supported their (often wrong) conclusion. They found it particularly humiliating when, in front of their colleagues, the attending physician would evaluate the patient, ask a few questions, and obtain the additional information that clearly if not known by the presenter, should have been known. This would generally lead to a discussion as to how faulty information is likely to produce incorrect results impacting the care of the patient. This may mean tests and procedures that were not really necessary, further producing confounding results as well as delaying those tests and procedures which would have led to the correct conclusion quicker. I have subsequently imparted General Dyke's guidance every time I have assumed responsibility over others, and this has served me well as a leader.

In my initial orientation from Colonel Vanderploog, he stressed to maintain a bias for positive action and choose your battles wisely. Going back to my infantry days, when planning an offensive operation, you attempt to choose the environment where you want to fight, draw the enemy into that position, and prepare the field with artillery and air support. Battles in business do not involve guns and bombs, but they may still be over turf or territory. Facts (not assumptions unless identified as such), probabilities, efficiencies, and words are the weapons of choice. Prepare the verbal battlefield. Study the problem thoroughly, identify the decision maker, feed him or her parcels of information beforehand, enlist your supporters, and pick a setting where the decision maker will have freedom of choice and not be tempted to "play to the bleachers" as can happen if one makes a proposal in front of an audience and the decision maker is not prepared to make a decision on the spot. The stronger the factual basis and the more information shared in advance to allow for internalization and reason, the greater the odds of achieving what you desire. Be prepared to execute promptly and vigorously upon approval and anticipate success. A positive approach is contagious.

From the onset, you must recognize the value of great employees. If you do not, they will find better options and the organization will have to replace them. This requires advertising, recruiting, assessing, hiring, and training. All of these consume time and are expensive. Therefore, you must understand what is important to employees and make sure that working in your organization meets these needs. Beyond a competitive salary, one of the biggest factors often is how the culture in the organization allows them or deters them from time for family and friends. Balance in life produces a better overall employee in the long term. This requires leaders to have the self-discipline to avoid having employees work overtime unless truly necessary for their mission and to compensate them appropriately when this happens. (Remember there are different rules in this regard for exempt versus non-exempt employees.) Further, you must be a role model in this regard. If they see you working weekends or staying late to "finish something up," they will feel obligated to do the same. When this leads to discord at home, you will find them seeking better, more family-friendly opportunities.

Another important lesson for me pertained to the difference between positive and negative leadership. I am almost embarrassed to share this particular lesson, as it was taught to me by my daughter's Netherland Dwarf rabbit, named Fluffy. He was banished to the back yard after my daughter let him play with my other daughter's house rabbit, Snowball, resulting in six additional rabbits to give to friends. Fluffy was safe when he was free in the yard during the day, but he needed to be in his cage at night to protect him from owls, large cats, and any other nocturnal pred-ator. To get him into the cage, the family would try to prod him in the right direction with long poles. The problem was that, when prodded, he would always jump, but not necessarily in the right direction, and it would take up to half an hour to drive him into the cage. After a few weeks of this, I noticed that when I was bringing a box of yogurt drops out to his cage, he hopped over there after me, as this was his favorite treat. Thereafter, we tried a new tactic. I would walk to the cage, shaking the box vigorously. I would toss some in, and he would rapidly follow and jump in the cage. My conclusion was that a negative stimulus would cause him to jump, but in a random direction—occasionally even back toward the source of the stimulus. However, with the positive stimulus, he always hopped in that direction. Reflecting on this, I realized that it was fair to extrapolate this behavior to people. Thus I developed this leadership philosophy: when I wanted action, I would always start with a positive stimulus and if that alone was insufficient, follow with a gentle negative stimulus, only sufficient to cause motion, followed quickly by a positive stimulus to give direction and keep on course.

An important part of my philosophy is summed up in this quote from J. Thomas May, Chairman and Chief Executive Officer of the Simmons First Foundation, and member of the Arkansas Blue Cross and Blue Shield Board of Directors, in *15 Elements for a Successful Career*: "Make sure your moral and ethical standards are aligned with those of your employer."

If your ethics are lower than the ethics of your employer, you will ultimately err in the application of your ethical standards and will not last with the organization. Similarly, if your ethical standards are higher, ultimately you will have to compromise your own ethical standards and potentially tarnish your reputation, or leave the organization before this happens.

It is crucial to realize that you really cannot ethically fail to act on what you do know and then pretend or hope others assume that you did not know. Further, there is no such thing as "plausible deniability." You do not protect yourself by pretending you did not know something, nor can you protect your leader by withholding key information. Recognize that for every wrong, there is always at least one person that sees it and at least one person that tells. Never be a party to a cover up. The truth always comes out eventually.

Every organization has a mission. Generally, in larger corporations, there is a clear mission statement crafted by the executive leadership, published in some format and required reading for all new employees. In smaller organizations, the mission may be implied or intuitively obvious. A corollary to making sure there is not an employer-employee ethical mismatch is to make sure that you understand and are comfortable with the stated or implied mission of the organization. Intrinsic to the mission of all large, for-profit corporations is the financial return to shareholders. Service to others may be a component of the mission of a for-profit organization, but this is always secondary to the financial return.

The primary mission of not-for-profit organizations is generally a societal benefit. An important component of my decision to join Blue Cross Blue Shield of Vermont and later Arkansas Blue Cross and Blue Shield was that these were not-for-profit health plans. In both organizations, I always acted with the societal mission in mind and felt that I was engaged in service to others.

As a leader you will have to make many decisions. Some decisions will be easy, others hard; for some, time will be critical, for others not. When time is less critical and the decision does not need to be immediate, I generally survey those that I lead and solicit suggestions. This phase, which I refer to as the discussion phase, should usually start with the more junior member of the team and work upward in order of seniority. It is important that all ideas be on the table and that all are taken seriously into consideration. The more input in this setting and at this time, the better the ultimate decision is likely to be. The next phase is the decision phase, which belongs to the decision-making authority, either an individual or a group.

When I am the decision-making authority I have always taken the approach that is outlined below and an extract of which is included in the Philosophy Memorandum in the appendix section. While I used this approach, it was my friend Colonel (later Major General) John S. Parker whose thoughts helped me to frame the words, as he expressed a very similar philosophy. Before making any significant decisions, whether at work or in my personal life, once the facts are settled, I mentally ponder the following five questions, in sequence, for if the answer is negative at any level, I will not move in that direction without remedying the issue. As you read through them, keep in mind that I consider morality, ethics, and integrity to be absolute values, and I encourage others never to lose their internal focus and think otherwise. At the end of our days, there is no better compliment than to be considered an honorable person in all regards. The five crucial questions are as follows:

Does this meet my sense of morality? This is personal, as morality means different things to different people, but mine is based in the Anglican faith in which I was raised. If I am contemplating anything and it does not meet my sense of morality, count me out.

Is this ethical? Considering whether something I do will deceive another or give me an unfair advantage over another, I will reframe my position in a way that does neither. Generally, I have found that by making certain adjustments, I can meet the general standards of ethical behavior, as well as my own.

Is this legal? Sometimes the answer is obvious, but sometimes it requires consultation with an attorney. I do not ask this until I have resolved the ethical question, as there are plenty examples of unethical but legal behaviors and I personally do not want to engage in this type of behavior, even if failure to do so is to my disadvantage.

What are the implications of this decision? Not only do I look at the direct effects, but I also seek and analyze likely second- and third-order effects, both those that are clearly direct consequences as well as those potentially unanticipated consequences of this decision. This does not mean that I will not proceed, but it does mean that I will be prepared for the consequences and have weighed them as to relative value.

Is this the right thing to do? Even after reviewing the first four considerations and doing a cost/benefit analysis, I still reflect one last time in a final mental summary to decide if what I plan is, in fact, the right thing to do under the current circumstances.

The final phase is the implementation phase, and the expectation is that once the decision has been made and all input considered, everyone involved will implement it as if it was their idea in the first place. Having the opportunity to provide input which is seriously considered, even if it differs from the final decision, does wonders to alleviate resistance, undermining, and passive-aggressive behavior at implementation.

It is important to share acclaim with the person who sparked an idea and the person or people who actually did the work. Without the work of these people, no leader can be successful. There is another old saying that applies here: it is amazing what you can achieve if you don't care who gets the credit.

To again refer to Colonel Vanderploog, in my initial orientation from him when I became the Commander, 3d Medical Battalion, he made it clear that errors in judgment and mistakes are permissible, even expected to a certain extent, but violations of trust are not. As a leader, you must be candid, forthright, and completely honest. There should always be an after-action review of any new initiative, and all should be free to engage in an open discussion. On more than one occasion, I have seen, and even been a party to, seemingly brilliant proposals that were professionally executed but had results that were nowhere near what was expected. However, with an open, non-threatening post-process review rather than a fault-finding activity, everyone involved learned from the episode and all were better for it in the long run. Sometimes the cost was worth the experience gained, but not always; some things had to be written off to a learning exercise. The added value of this approach is that once there has been investment in the wrong venture, the after-action review makes it much easier to halt that effort and move on to a new opportunity, rather than perpetuate a losing program in order to avoid embarrassment.

One should also understand and communicate both that it is easier to do things correctly the first time (and not the third or fourth) and that bad news almost inevitably becomes worse news over time and surprises are not welcome in these instances. You must let your leader know immediately when things go wrong, and you must insist that those you lead do the same for you. Never "shoot the messenger" in this setting or you will stop or reduce future negative messages and be blindsided at some point in the future. Likewise, never tell someone to do the impossible so that you can "wash your hands of it" and shift the blame.

Courtesy is a tremendous tool. This is illustrated in the four options below for how to ask for a special report:

- Run this report.
- I need you to run this report.
- Please run this report.

- This is an important report because... Please review this and bring me a report that will allow me to make the right decision.

It should be obvious which of these will lead to the best report and produce the right decision. Further, remember to offer thanks and give feedback as to how the report was used. This will give you even better reports going forward.

The issue of leadership style often surfaces. For example, some leaders are quiet and unassuming; others are flamboyant and easily gather admirers. The important concept is to be yourself and be consistent. There are multiple leadership styles that will work for one but not for another; do not role-play unless you are a highly skilled actor.

Two famous contrasting styles from World War II were the quiet and unassuming manner of General Omar Bradley (known as the soldier's soldier), and the flamboyant appearance and actions of General George S. Patton. Both men were highly successful.

It is well known in history, and readily apparent from their appearance in historical photos (and the movie *Patton*) that Generals Bradley and Patton had almost the complete opposite leadership styles, yet when you read their instructions for future leaders they are actually fairly synchronous on many points.

General Bradley (*Leadership Strategy Insider*, September 9, 2011):
- Engage but don't draw attention to yourself.
- Demand peak performance from direct reports.
- Protect achievers when they get into trouble.
- Get rid of marginal performers.
- Disagree with people discreetly.
- Don't let your ego get out of control.
- Spend time "in the field" but do it without grandstanding.

General Patton's Ten Commandments (Army Live—Official Blog of U.S. Army)
- Do everything that you ask of those you command.
- Say what you mean, and mean what you say.
- Do not fear failure.
- Do more than is required of you.

- Do not take counsel of your fears.
- Always go forward.
- Take calculated risks.
- Give credit where it is due.
- Accept full responsibility for the actions of yourself and your men.

Most of the organizations that I have mentioned in this narrative are no longer in the active Army. This includes the 11th LIB and Americal Division from Vietnam, the 193d INF BDE from the Canal Zone, LAMC and Fort Ord from California, the 8ID, 3d MED BN, and VII Corps from Europe, and the AIT BDE from Alabama. Nevertheless, they are still part of the Army. Their colors, lineage, honors, and history remain at the Institute of Heraldry in Washington DC, ready to be returned to the active Army should our country need them. The same is true for me and my fellow military retirees. We are still a part of our country's military force subject to recall to active duty in a time of need, as many were during Operations Desert Shield and Storm, though on an individual basis the probability for my peer group grows slimmer every year as we age, yet those of us in good health would step up in a heartbeat.

During my career with the Army and my time at the Arkansas and Vermont Blue Cross and Blue Shield organizations, whether I served in a staff or a leadership position, I took great pride in the organization and did everything in my power to leave it better than it was when I arrived. At first, I had a sense of regret that any legacy that I left would have been miniscule. Then I realized that as a leader, the legacy that I left was not the organization but rather the people who had served with me and whatever lessons they carried forward from our service together. Of greater importance than any institutional legacy is that I have been a mentor for numerous evolving leaders, and my true legacy is what they learned from me, how they used this advice, and what they passed on to the leaders that followed them.

Given the way the world and society change over time, I have concluded that the influence people have on others is the only real legacy anyone leaves. If these lessons are, in turn, passed on to others, the legacy may live on for generations. It matters not that I do not know the people who mentored my leaders and those I mentored really do not know the people know who mentored me. The legacy remains no matter who takes credit and when they do so. I have tremendous pride in those that I have mentored, many of whom have gone farther in their careers than I, yet remain in touch with me and share their accomplishments with me. It is impossible to state how proud I am for them.

Finally, it is important to understand the need for, and value of, community service. I was raised to serve, not just in the military, but in the community as well. We all live in a community, and my wife Ann and I believe strongly that you cannot be neutral in a community—you either give to it or you take from it—and we choose to give. Our appreciation of community service primarily was derived from Boy and Girl Scouting, and I served as a scoutmaster before I had sons old enough to be Boy Scouts, and Ann assisted with the Girl Scout program at Fort Sill, Oklahoma. I served as a scoutmaster in the Canal Zone before I had a son old enough to participate, and when I left Vermont I was the chairman of the Long Trail District even though my youngest was off in college. Ann, too, worked with Girl Scouts at several locations, but made her greatest contributions with the American Red Cross, including serving as hospital chairman for volunteer service, providing nursing education to military families in Europe, and ultimately serving as the chairman for District III of the American Red Cross in Europe. In Vermont, she served on two school boards and the board for the senior center.

It should be noted by emerging leaders that many companies, large and small, take great pride in and even advertise the community service of their employees and leaders. Increasing visibility in community service is often an understood, but unwritten, criterion for civilian leadership at an executive level.

Finally, for those of us blessed with children, they are our most important legacy. My siblings and I are my parents' legacy, and our children are the legacy of Ann and me. As of today, we have a son who is a busy CPA, but also a youth soccer coach who effectively built the youth soccer program in Panama City Beach to what it is today. One daughter is an Air Force lawyer (JAG) who was one of the first "Special Victims Counsels" and the other is a Doctor of Audiology who has assisted many with adapting to newly acquired hearing or recovering hearing lost. Our son is an Army Reserve Captain with a prior tour as an Infantry Officer in Afghanistan who is now a Civil Affairs Officer working on a PhD related to education enhancement in developing countries; he is currently preparing for another overseas deployment to foster military-civilian partnerships for the common good.

For you who have taken the time to read this work, thank you, but now the next steps are up to you. If you are reading this, your profession is or will likely become leadership. If so, embark on a life-long study of this role. There are a lot of teaching points covered here, but I have attempted to design this in a way that you can come back to it and review and add those you find pertinent to your own leadership philosophy and style. There are many books on the market, and I recommend that you continue a reading program on leadership. I also urge you to pick wisely what you choose to read, think about what the authors say, and before you adopt an idea, be sure that you agree it is a good fit for you. Observe and analyze those who lead you and others. Ask yourself what makes great leaders great, okay leaders simply okay, and bad leaders bad.

Finally, develop and maintain your own "Leadership Journal" and document your observations. Review it from time to time. Occasionally, these notes may pull you back if you drift off track from where you want to be.

I sincerely hope that what I have written will help you to succeed and to inspire others, and that you will have a well-earned sense of pride in those that follow you.

Appendix 1:

Brigadier General Griffin's Vision Statement for the Southeast Army Regional Medical Command, July 1997:

The Southeast Army Regional Health System will remain ready to support America's warfighting capability at home and abroad. Based around Eisenhower Army Medical Center and integrating all components of America's Army, our success depends upon earning and maintaining the confidence and respect of the supported installations and major commands. We will be known for individual and collective readiness and training, the promotion of wellness through community outreach programs, a large integrated primary care base, and easily accessible specialty care services. We will leverage the latest and the best of evolving technology to reach these goals. Our focus in all relationships will be consideration of others, both fellow military and civilian staff members and our patients. Our staff members will feel comfortable and thrive in our workplaces. We will demonstrate concern and compassion and we will preserve human dignity as we meet the needs of our patients. We will be good stewards of the nation's resources and a valued leader in the healthcare profession, profession of arms, and the U.S. Army Medical Command.

Appendix 2:

Dr. Griffin's Philosophy Memorandum, Arkansas Blue Cross and Blue Shield, November, 2010:

With the recent organizational changes, I think it would be useful to share my general philosophy with you all. I have held a variety of leadership positions over my careers, and have developed a way of doing business that works for me. By sharing my thoughts with you, I hope it will make it easier to work together and produce the highest value for our groups, our members, and our organization. Some of you have heard many of these points from me before and you likely will again. This is not an all-inclusive document, but rather it is a framework for future discussions...

I believe in the old adage that discipline means doing what is right, even when no one is looking. This entails integrity, teamwork, loyalty, communication, and initiative. I expect absolute integrity and I will deliver the same to you. We work as a team, we succeed together or we falter together. I expect each of you to help share a balanced load. Loyalty is critical in our dealings with each other, but also applies to our dealings with our members, groups, and providers. Talk to each other—share ideas and develop the best solutions. I don't think I've ever seen an area with too much communication, but I've seen several instances where there was too little communications resulting in some rather unpleasant surprises. Finally, when appropriate, take the initiative. If you know what is right, act on that knowledge in a timely manner and then let us work out the details later.

I handle decision making by first pondering five questions, and, if satisfied with the general merits, I then look at the business case analysis. You may wish to adopt this yourself, but certainly, you should ask yourselves these five questions before you bring an issue to me. These considerations are as follows:

Is it moral? Morality is often a personal view based upon an individual's value set, but if I feel that I am bumping up against my concept of morality, I look for other possibilities. I am, however, careful not to impose my individual sense of morality on others who may not have an identical value set.

Is it ethical? Morality and ethics are two different concepts and often it is easier to get consensus as to what is or isn't ethical behavior. For example, deceit usually is not considered immoral behavior, but it generally is unethical. If I think a proposal is unethical, I will seek alternatives that can produce the same (or better) results in an ethical manner. Of particular note is that I insist that individuals working with me in a clinical based role have the ability to and adhere to the ethical standards required by their individual professions.

Is it legal? In these days of healthcare reform, this is an even bigger question than it has been in the past. If you have any doubt, seek guidance from our corporate counsel before you bring a proposal forward. I do not operate in the grey area of questionable legality and encourage you all to do the same.

What are the consequences of this action? Decisions may have political consequences, they may result in relationship issues with members, providers, or groups, they may reduce our competitiveness in our industry, and they may produce desirable or undesirable second- or third-order effects. We need to look down the road to fully understand the consequences of our actions.

Is this the right thing to do?

Our industry has undergone tremendous transformation during the span of my career. Today, health insurance is looked upon much less like true insurance and much more like a collective health services purchasing program or cooperative. Businesses purchasing our services look to us to actively manage the health and healthcare needs of their employees while controlling overall healthcare costs. We must be equally diligent in managing the healthcare needs of our individual members where we are at risk for their healthcare costs. We must insist upon high standards of quality, evidence based, and cost effective clinical decision making.

Going into the future, this transformation will ultimately result in the sharing of this responsibility with our network providers. As this occurs, we must build strong partnerships. To do so, we must evaluate and to the extent possible, eliminate requirements that have been levied on the majority of practices to preclude aberrant behaviors by small minorities of practices that the majority wouldn't even consider. We have been actively reducing this burden, and to the extent possible, I would like to continue to roll it back over the coming years.

As a corporation, we are expected to provide coverage in accordance with our certificates and primary coverage criteria. Our criteria are readily available, and most, though not all, providers have been thoughtful in providing treatment to our members. Accordingly, we should approach problem issues or claims with an approach that seeks a legitimate reason to provide benefits, and be consistent in denying benefits where no such reason exists. Where the needs of our members fall outside of our certificates we should be active in assisting these members with leveraging community support to meet their needs.

There is a strong relationship between fitness and productivity. In addition, as a health plan we support wellness as a part of the solution to escalating healthcare costs. I encourage everyone to join me in setting the example to the rest of the company in promoting wellness. You should take time to exercise to the extent that you are physically able; participate in health assessment and improvement activities; comply with preventive medicine guidelines for evaluation and screening for your age and gender; and get your flu shot annually. If the clinical experts in the company do not do this, how can we expect the non-clinical people to do so?

Together, we have a great opportunity to create a better and healthier future, improve the health-related behavior of our members, support our individual and institutional providers, and strengthen business by keeping healthcare costs in check. Together, we have the collective ability to do more good for more people than we ever would have on an individual basis.

CPSIA information can be obtained
at www.ICGtesting.com
Printed in the USA
BVHW092240120219
540124BV00001B/1/P